P9-ELT-044

Best Wishes

Mrs. Williams

May God Bless you always

Annita Lee
10/10/2009
Proverbs 3:5&6

# A Voice to Be Heard

Reaching Youth and Keeping Them
Reached in the 21st Century

## Connita Lee

authorHOUSE®

*AuthorHouse™*
*1663 Liberty Drive*
*Bloomington, IN 47403*
*www.authorhouse.com*
*Phone: 1-800-839-8640*

*© 2009 Connita Lee. All rights reserved.*

*No part of this book may be reproduced, stored in a retrieval system, or transmitted by any means without the written permission of the author.*

*First published by AuthorHouse 6/2/2009*

*ISBN: 978-1-4389-7925-0 (sc)*

*Printed in the United States of America*
*Bloomington, Indiana*

*This book is printed on acid-free paper.*

*Unless otherwise indicated, all Scripture quotations are taken from the King James version of the Bible.*

*Cover design by Michelle Morris*

# Contents

# ACKNOWLEDGMENTS

To God our Father who spoke to my heart six years ago and said: *A Voice to Be Heard*. He allowed me to begin to write and write and write until this project was completed. I dedicate this book to God, our Heavenly Father. I would also like to thank my many supporters, especially Cherese A. Cadet of Hampton, GA, Lorraine Cooper of Chicago, IL, JoAnn Claytor—my sister and friend—of Memphis, TN, Michelle Morris of Chicago, IL, who heard the vision and used her gifted hands to create a beautiful book cover. To all of these people who gave me the finishing touches for *A Voice to Be Heard*, and the many more who prayed for me, I say to you: Thank you.

To Anike Hogan for her obedience to God while obeying His word by demonstrating through Ezekiel 34:26-27 "A Shower of Blessings!" To Pastor Yvonne Lee Wilson and Elder Tanda Adams, whose words of wisdom and help in regards to the "*Straight Talk Strategy*," encouraged me to complete the task at hand. To Elder Catherine Evans, who spoke directly to my spirit man and encouraged me to stay FOCUSED on the task at hand: our youth.

To Elder-Elect Kim L. Petty, author of *An Encounter with God*, for pushing me to get the job done. To Pastor Therese B. Turner who trusted and believed in the vision and the missionary, and paid for five books in advance!

Thank you all for your unwavering love and support. From one author to another: Just do it. For God can; and He will make a way. Just keep believing and trusting in His word.

To Faith Lutheran Church, New Vision of Faith Ministries, New Vision of Faith Fellowship, The House of Prayer for All Nations Ministries, and all the other Ministries who allow me to help impart and impact their youth ministry groups over the years: Thank you.

A special thank you to my mother, (MEMA) Marguerite E. Lee-Walker, who has always taught us to do what is right through the Eyes of God and to keep our name honorable. To my siblings and all of my family members: Thank you for always supporting me in every task that was upon me to do for the Kingdom of God. The support of a family is important to every believer and especially the family of Faith. May God's Blessings be upon you one hundred fold.

# FOREWORD & WORDS OF ENCOURAGEMENT

Elder Connita Lee has been used by God in youth ministry for well over 25 years. *A Voice To Be Heard* is a must read for leaders in the 21st century church, from a tried and tested vessel of God. The practical strategies and concepts will help you to bridge the generational divide and provide a vehicle to rescue children and teens from the grip of Satan.

I know the results first hand of what Elder Lee outlines in this manual. I was her student and am now her Pastor, and I can testify that this ministry works and is needed around the world to reach this generation.

--Apostle David A. Rodgers, Senior Pastor
The House of Prayer for All Nations Ministries

We are living in a time where Christian ministry has been minimized by compromise. We have minimized Christian ministry by assuming the generational divide cannot be crossed. Many adult Christian leaders have failed to embrace young people *"where they are at"* to ensure the life of that ministry. Though a great many things have been done around the world to further the Gospel of Jesus Christ we have not maximized our efforts by including young people in the ministry activity. We have not realized the full scope of youthful involvement to further the legacy of Christian ministry. Young people are *A Voice to Be Heard* in every congregation and ministry. It would be wise for adults to embrace that voice in wisdom to guide it in the right direction.

--Apostle Kevin E. Dean, Senior Pastor
New Vision of Faith Ministries

*To my sister, A Voice to Be Heard* is a testament to you making full proof of your ministry. You have always demonstrated the love of God to the youth. Your excitement and enthusiasm motivates them to experience God more and more. This book is just a portion of your life in the youth ministry, and the awesome impact that you have had on the young people. This book will be a blessing to everyone who reads it and desires to grow their ministries. God will do a great work in and through the youth to build the kingdom. I encourage you to continue to press toward the mark of the high calling in Christ Jesus. Be encouraged and blessed in all God has in store for you and the youth in the 21ˢᵗ century. God Bless You and I love you.

--Pastor Therese B. Turner
Living the Resurrected Life Ministries

*A Voice to Be Heard* is an awesome snapshot of a lifetime of love for and understanding of children. Every page boldly proclaims a love for the Lord and the special gift of being able to see into the hearts of young people and bring them into the love of God. Elder Lee's passion and compassion for all children comes through in every word. With a no-nonsense approach, solid advice, and simple ideas to get the church and children "*on fire for the Lord*," Elder Lee has written a powerful tool for the youth ministries of the world to move forth confidently into the 21ˢᵗ century!

--Cherese A. Vines
YA fiction author

# INTRODUCTION

This book, *A Voice to Be Heard* is birthed out of many years of being a Servant and a Dedicated Youth Leader to several youth ministry groups.

Our youth ministry was geared toward youth in the body of Christ, and especially toward those who were outside the body of Christ, encouraging them to come together and work through a Straight Talk strategy.

Our youth must be trained and allowed to function in ways that our generation was never allowed to do within the church of the past. Embracing changes in this 21st century church will cause a move of God in this generation like never before, that will spread throughout the world with young people who are on fire for Him, going out into the highways and byways to compel young people to demonstrate the Love of God through Christ Jesus our Lord. To God Be the Glory!

# OUR MISSION
# OUR VISION
# OUR GOALS

Proverbs 22:6 *"Train up a child in the way he should go and when he is old he will not depart from it."*

Mark 1:3 *"The voice of one crying in the wilderness, prepare ye the way of the Lord, make his path straight."*

## OUR MISSION

To Train, Educate, and Encourage youth so that they may empower each other to live positive and productive lives.

## OUR VISION

To develop youth leadership by fully equipping them with the skills to reach a generation of Future Leaders. Our youth will be able to connect with their peers in ways we cannot imagine. God's Army is geared toward building youth centers for all youth to come and be made whole.

# OUR GOALS

To provide a safe environment for youth to gather where they will develop positive peer relationships and be mentored to lead a successful life.

To provide faith-based opportunities for youth to grow socially, academically, artistically, and culturally.

To provide experiences for youth to gain ownership by helping them develop skills for exceptional leadership and healthy decision-making.

To provide positive role models to encourage and impact our future leaders so that they may reach their greatest potential in this 21st Century of believers.

# Part I

# YOUTH MINISTRY

- WHAT IS YOUTH MINISTRY?
- A GREATER VISION: *"Reaching Youth and Keeping Them Reached"* in the 21st Century
- FUTURE LEADERS IN THE 21ST CENTURY
- YOUTH LEADERSHIP TEAM
- SEEING BEYOND WHAT YOUR EYES CAN SEE
- KIDS ARE PEOPLE TOO

# Youth Ministry

Youth Ministry plays an invaluable part in the Church ministry. There are several ministries, or categories, within the youth ministry. The Board of Directors will plan and set up the different ministries within the Youth Ministry Department. First of all, a youth director is appointed by the pastor and the board of directors. This individual should have a serious background in the ministry and have a great love for children. Let me say that again. **This individual should have a great love for the children.**

When dealing with a youth ministry, there must be committed people working in this department. A lot of times, people get into a ministry for the recognition and not necessarily to help the youth. They soon find out that it's really not for them. The Word of God says test the spirit by the spirit. 1 John 4:1 – "*Beloved, believe not every spirit, but try the spirits whether they are of God: because many false prophets are gone out into the world.*" Matthew 7:24 – *Therefore whosoever heareth these sayings of mine, and doeth them, I will liken him unto a wise man, which built his house upon a rock.*

Use wise judgment on selecting a youth director and youth workers. Never take anyone for granted; hear what he/she says and hear what he/she is *not* saying. In other words, leaders sharpen your discernment. The youth director must be led by the Spirit of God; and you will see your youth ministry prosper like never before.

After the youth director is chosen, they will need to seek God's guidance when they begin to organize the youth ministry. Order is the key first; and then the purpose, the process, and the priority. Write the vision and make it plain (Habakkuk 2:2). Once the youth department is in order, get ready for the Manifestation of God to reveal itself.

The youth director should pray and pray and pray some more until he/she knows the direction that God is taking the youth ministry; because as director, he/she will appoint minister leaders in the different age groups and programs under the youth department. Choosing the right youth helpers is a vital step. It is so important to know them that labor among you (1 Thessalonians 5:12).

Communication and knowledge is also important in developing an effective Youth Ministry Department. The Word of God says my people perish for the lack of knowledge (Hosea 4:6). Everything that we do, we must do it unto God and His Son Jesus—who is the Author and the Finisher of our FAITH (Hebrews 12:2).

Once the youth director and youth workers are in place, the next step is to develop programs within the ministry. It is important to take the time to learn who our youth are and use this knowledge to shape our ministries. We don't want to have areas in our ministry that are not effective. If our youth like to dance, we need to create a Praise Dance Ministry. If our youth like to sing, we should create a choir dedicated to them. A Drama Ministry is also a good option. It gives youth an avenue to express themselves. It is important to get input from them on what they want to do. When they feel they are a part of it, they will put every effort into making the ministry a success. It's their ministry, let them help shape it.

We are raising up an ARMY for the Lord. If we impart wisdom into the lives of these young people, we will see an explosion in our youth department that can be seen all over the world.

# What is Youth Ministry?

Youth Ministry is just like any other ministry in the Body of Christ. It is to prepare the youth of any church to be ready to operate in any office or board that is represented in the churches today.

For instance, if our church is operating in Intercessory Prayer, has an Ushers Board or a Greeter Ministry, a Watchmen Ministry, a Deacon Board, an Evangelist Ministry, a Prophetic Ministry, or a Help Ministry, our youth need to be trained in every one of those areas to fulfill the great commission that is given to us by our Heavenly Father (Matthew 28:19-20). Our youth want nothing more than to represent and be a part of the ministry that they are being trained in. Remember, they too desire to have a *Voice to be Heard.*

We must realize that it is essential to train the next generation as warriors, even allowing them to preach the Word of God. Our youth must be able to function in ways that we were never allowed to do in our churches when we were growing up. This is a new day, and old things that worked in a previous time will not work today with this generation. We must be kingdom-minded and help raise a generation who will also be kingdom-minded in order to hear the Voice of God and to move and make it happen. It is all about winning souls for the Kingdom of God.

It's time for the Body of Christ to embrace the changes that God has put before us in this 21st century—to fight the good fight of FAITH with the power and authority given to us through our Lord and Savior Jesus Christ.

Having a youth ministry to embrace prepares our youth to be future leaders in the Body of Christ. It also brings a great sense of worth to youth when they know that they can participate in their church or youth group. Our older teens can help train junior teens on the various duties within the different ministries. Our ministry can then reach beyond the four walls of our church building and out into the communities where a greater impact can be achieved. Remember, junior teens are not as mature, but our teens can help them prepare for an experience that can change their lives forever.

# A Greater Vision: *Reaching Youth and Keeping Them Reached* in the 21ST Century

It is so important to build and establish a relationship with young people. We gain their unconditional love and trust when we are real and honest with them. In today's society, our youth are faced with many more obstacles than we faced growing up. Crime is at an all time high, teen pregnancy, date rape, incest, drugs, and alcohol—the list goes on and on. While we may have had some of these same challenges, they are much more prevalent in the lives of today's youth. It takes a village and a community to raise a child. In reaching the youth of today, the impartation will encourage them to reach their peers.

REACH, BUILD, and TRUST are three key words to get the flow going in any youth ministry group. We must REACH out to our youth to bring them into the knowledge of Christ. They will not be able to make it in this world without the knowledge, love, grace, and mercy of our Lord and Savior Jesus Christ. It is our job as youth leaders to help them get there. We must BUILD a solid relationship with them so they will know there is always a support system for them whenever they need it. We cannot be judgmental in our approach, but open and honest without being compromising. Youth need to know that what they share will be taken seriously; and they will not be looked down on or judged. Most importantly, we must develop a TRUST relationship with our young charges. They must be absolutely sure they have our confidence. If we break that, it may be a long time, if ever, before they will confide in us again.

Developing a Children's, Junior, and Teen ministry is very important. This affords them the opportunity to express themselves. We must remember that kids are people too; and STOP, LOOK, AND LISTEN before we voice our opinion. We need the young, the old, and the mature to reach this world with the Gospel of Jesus Christ. Learn to hear the cry of our youth today.

We need to be careful and STOP talking so much. Sometimes we get caught up in lecturing our youth when we may have started off just giving them some sound advice. We need to LOOK at their behavior. Their actions and interactions with each other can tell us a lot about what's going on with them or what they need. Take the time to just sit back and watch what's going on with your youth. It is imperative that we LISTEN to what our youth are saying. Since we've "been there and done that," we may think we have all the answers. Listen to your youth and really understand what they are saying. They know when you've listened to them and when you have not.

Let's take a closer look at some of the many things that can be implemented into our churches' youth ministry. First, don't be afraid of making changes; without change and a vision the ministry will die. Proverbs 29:18 – "*Where there is no vision, the people perish...*" We must first get a plan in place. Assess the needs of our youth and determine what they need. We have to know our young people: their character, their passions, etc. before we can truly help them. We have to meet youth where they are. We cannot design a ministry based on where we want it to go. It has to be geared towards what they need.

Jesus said let the dead bury the dead (Matthew 8:22). Take heed to this saying. If it doesn't work, that means it may be dead. Take a closer look at what you're currently doing in your ministry and see if it works. If it does, improve upon it. If it doesn't, get rid of it and try something else. Try not to become stagnate or predictable in your ministry. Don't be afraid to try something new. Challenge yourself to think outside the traditional way of doing things. You never know what may put a spark in your youth. However, be careful. We don't want to fall into the trap of conforming to the world's way of capturing our youth. We want to instill in our youth that they can have fun without losing who they are in Christ. It only takes two to three young people to make a difference in our church. Train them and we can get an army for the Lord. Young people will evangelize to each other without even knowing it.

**What is Evangelism?** Evangelism is the act of announcing the "*Good News*" of a risen Savior. It is an opportunity to share with humanity that sin separates us from God, but through faith in Jesus Christ His death, burial, and resurrection, they can be saved and experience a true relationship with God. Daniel 12:3 – "*Those who lead many to righteousness will shine like the stars forever and ever.*" 2 Timothy 4:5 – "*Do the work of an evangelist...*" 1 Peter 3:15 – "*...be ready always to give an answer to every man that asketh you a reason of the hope that is in you with meekness and fear...*"

Also, our body language plays an important part in communicating with youth. We can either except them or reject them by our reaction to their outward appearance. We should not "judge a book by its cover." Get to know your youth first and see what their needs are. A small kindness from you can go a long way.

Next, get people involved who have a love for young people and who are also not afraid to discipline. Young people will "try" us, because that's what they do; but we must take a stand. Stand on the Word of God and make a difference in the lives of our youth. Kids love it when we demonstrate the Love of God. We must be an example of Christ so that they are following Christ and not us.

# Future Leaders in

# the 21ST Century

Now is the time to train our Future Leaders in the Body of Christ. The church must be willing and able to train these 21st century leaders.

If we do not invest in our youth and impact their lives, the church will be in trouble. Without future leaders in the Body of Christ, no future churches can reach out beyond their four walls. We must understand that the body gets older, and without new parts coming in to be equipped and trained and sent out, the body will die without fulfilling the great commission as told in Matthew 28:19-20.

Will the church remain in the wilderness until everyone has died off because we failed to train and impact the next generation for leadership? Our youth are searching for something to fill the emptiness of their lives. The void is not being filled in the ministry because of self-gain and fame in the Body of Christ. God is a waiting for His sons and daughters to awake and fulfill the mission that He has given them. How long will we continue to deny the youth their part in the Body of Christ when it comes to leadership? The Word of God says that a child shall lead them. Isaiah 11:6 – "*The wolf also shall dwell with the lamb, and the leopard shall lie down with the kid; and the calf and the young lion and the fatling together; and a little child shall lead them.*"

If the Body of Christ refuses to help train future leaders, God will raise up a generation that will be Spirit-led by Him to accomplish what He already told the body to conquer.

We must be able to discern our future leaders, target them with training, and encourage them to take their rightful places in the Body of Christ, or this generation will be lost forever without hope or worth in this world. In spite of what the enemy (the evil one) is trying to do in their lives, we must continue to speak those things that "*be not as thou they were*" in the life of every youth in the Body of Christ. Romans 4:17 – "*As it is written, I have made thee a father of many nations,) before him whom he believed, even God, who quickeneth the dead, and calleth those things which be not as though they were.*"

Future leaders should be able to produce after their own kind to ensure that the Body of Christ will go forth with power and authority. Future leaders must operate with compassion and a willingness to go the extra mile in reaching the lost at any cost.

Future leaders will not be afraid of the arrows by night or the sinners by day (Psalm 91), but remain FOCUSED on the promises of what is written in the Word of God. They must believe that we are more than conquerors (Romans 8:37), and remember we can do all things through Christ that strengthen us (Philippians 4:13).

Empower your future leaders in this 21st century, to take a stand and go forth with the power and authority that was given to all believers in His name. What is the name that is above all names? Jesus Christ our Lord.

Pray for all future leaders that they will impact and impart the Heart of Christ to others with love and compassion. Please remember that not just anyone will do, for we need committed saints of God who will empower future leaders through the Goodness of God that is in their lives. Take a stand and develop leaders for the 21st century to do exceeding and abundantly above all that we can ask or think in a world that is so desperately in need.

What legacy are we imparting in our future leaders to impact and empower this dying world? No hope, no power. More hope, more power. The time is now to raise a generation of future leaders to impact this world with the Gospel of Jesus Christ our Lord.

# Youth Leadership Team

Philippians 4:6 - "*Be careful for nothing, but in everything by prayer and supplication with thanksgiving let your requests be made known unto God.*" When seeking youth leaders and developing teams, we must be prayerful and watchful in allowing God to show us the individuals He designed to help reach the world.

Youth are looking for something to do in the Body of Christ. So many of them feel like they do not belong or that there is really nothing for them to do in the church today. The Youth Leadership Team can help each youth identify their gifts and potential to have a positive impact in the Body of Christ. Many of our youth today just want to belong to something, whether it is good or bad.

Investing in one youth can reach thousands. The Bible says that one can chase a thousand but two can put ten thousands to flight (Deuteronomy 32:30). We must ask God to help us see the leadership in our youth. God, by His Holy Spirit, will lead and guide us to make the right choice. There is nothing too hard or impossible for our God. It is so important to make our youth a part of this next Move of God in the last days, so our youth leadership groups should be a great concern for the Body of Christ.

Each day, too many of our youth die physical and spiritual deaths without cause. Without a vision, the people will perish. Let's not forget that kids are people too. We must begin to train this generation with the Word of God. Let's take control and develop their minds, using the Word to apply hope, love, peace, and joy to win this generation back for Christ to use in a mighty way.

Remember to get the input of your youth. Everyone has their own personality. Make sure to inform each future leader that this is not about them, but about winning souls by any means necessary through Christ who strengthens them (Philippians 4:13).

It is important to get five teams of leadership started, for this represents the Five Fold Ministry Ephesians 4:11 – "*It was he who gave some to be (1) apostles, some to be (2) prophets, some to be (3) evangelists, and some to be (4) pastors and (5) teachers.*" Try to put one strong-willed youth in each leadership team. Every team will be over a particular task and will be held accountable in whatever area they have been placed. Remember to pray and seek God for every team operation. Set the goals for each team and hold them accountable for planning programs, events, and projects.

Allow each youth leadership team to be over the Youth Service each month. Each team should be expected to develop the strategy and plans given to them by their youth leader. They must be willing to conduct monthly meetings to plan and accomplish all youth activities held in their church or events outside the church.

Before each program or event, each team will be held accountable for setting a standard by opening up with prayer and having a scripture reading. Each of these future leaders must have a prayer life. While we can have fun at the same time, we must not forget the main objective is winning souls for Christ in addition to developing our future leaders. Once each team finishes their devotion period, an open discussion with all teams should take place. Each team will be assigned a specific task to discuss: i.e. decorations, speakers, food, etc. Then every team will go into separate team meetings.

The designated leader from each team will serve as facilitator and lead their team's discussion session. They will brainstorm for ideas on how to accomplish their task. When everything has been addressed, all teams will reassemble for an open forum. During the open discussion, each youth team member will have at least 3 to 5 minutes to present their concerns or ideas on how to make the program or event a better affair.

Having teams work together is a big part of every event or program becoming a great success in winning souls for God. Remember there is one body but many members that work together on one accord. Always allow the youth leadership team to have the opportunity to lay the foundation of the programs and events. However, they must understand that they, along with the youth director and counselors make the final decisions together.

To have a successful youth leadership team, make sure all guidelines, rules, and regulations are known by your youth so they will have structure to their meeting. Every team should be prepared to present the Gospel to the lost. So make sure you have trained and equipped each team to reach their peers. Most importantly, they should be equipped to train others in their youth groups to become witnesses for Christ.

If we do not take the time to develop Youth Leadership Teams, and train our youth, we will be in a world of chaos. Everyone will go their own way and do whatever pleases them instead of what pleases God; and no one will be there to take a stand to follow the Word of God. Where are the true leaders in the Body of Christ to lead the lost to eternity?

# Seeing Beyond What Your Eyes Can See

Many times, we look on the outward appearance of our youth and are not able to see beyond it. Because our own sin can blind us from the truth, we need to focus on the relationship God has planned for us since the foundation of the world. If we will only imagine what God wants us to see, we will never look at any negative thing that will cause us to fail. God will give us the vision of where He wants us to be in our life's journey. God gave Father Abraham a vision to see beyond what he could see with his natural eye. He had the faith to carry out the vision to become the father of many nations. Like Abraham, we should seek God to help us see beyond the natural into the spiritual when dealing with our youth.

Well, how do we see beyond what our eyes can see? We must establish a relationship with God. We cannot be of any use to our youth or to God without knowing who He is and what He wants us to do. When we believe and put our trust in God, then we will grow in wisdom, knowledge, and obedience as we continue to seek His face. Our discernment will grow spiritually so that we can begin to see beyond what our natural eyes *cannot* see, into what our spiritual eyes *can* see.

Abraham trusted God enough to leave his father's house and go to a land which God had prepared for him and his people (Genesis 12:1). Although he had no idea where he was going or what he would encounter when he got there, Abraham trusted and believed enough in his God to obey Him and go. We have to do the same. You may not know what lies ahead in your youth ministry. Trust and believe that God knows what lies ahead; and if we only trust Him and seek His will, we will be able to see beyond the negative, the obstacles, the nay-sayers, and the fear. We must learn to look beyond what we can naturally see; but through the eyes of God (spiritual eyes), see into the lives of our youth and help them develop a strategy, so that we can impart the Word and trust the vision and plan that God has for them. If we don't, we will inherit a lost generation full of hopelessness.

What better way to serve God than by doing what He has given us in His word to do? Be like NIKE... *Just do it.* Take the walk of faith and receive the "promised" land full of milk and honey. Are you willing to see beyond what your eyes can see? We must not doubt the will and plan for our lives or the lives of our youth; for God has said it and it is so. We must be committed to the Body of Christ and to our youth.

If everyone encourages each other in the Body of Christ to go forth boldly into the promises of God and posses the land, what an awesome thing to see beyond what we can see in the natural and see into the spiritual realm. Stand on the Word of God and believe what it says. Your youth ministry will prosper and grow because you are not alone. Philippians 4:13 gives us the assurance we need: "*I can do all things through Christ which strengthens me.*"

It is time for the Body of Christ to take the faith walk and do the Will of the Father who sent us into the world, and take it by force with the Gospel of Jesus Christ. Are you ready? Then go forth with power and authority and posses the land; it's ours.

# Kids Are People Too

Sometimes in our life's journey we forget that we were once children waiting to be heard. Kids watch everything we do and say. We must learn to set an example for our children.

A    **K** ID
        **I** S
        **D** EFINITELY
        **S** PECIAL

Although kids are little ones that need guidance and direction, we must realize that they are in a learning pattern that can cause them to either achieve in life or fail. Encouraging our children is vitally important in their daily lives. It can be the difference between success and failure - God's saving grace and Satan's fiery furnace. Speaking positive things to our youth will help build their character.

Our Apostle will say: "You see an ugly child, follow him or her home and something ugly will open the door." Don't get me wrong; while that may be funny to some, ugliness can start from the inside out. This can change the disposition of kids and have a negative impact on them for the rest of their life's journey.

If we continue to keep the mindset that kids are to be seen and not heard, we will stop our children literally from reaching the great potential and plan God ordained for them from the beginning of the world.

If we believe God's Word is true and that He heard the cry of His children when Pharaoh would not let them go, then why do we think that the voice of *our children* is different? God heard the cries of His children and did something about it. God hears and answers the voices of His children today, but He wants us to be obedient to His word. When our children cry out, it should be the same as when we call on our Heavenly Father. We need to do something about it. We are to demonstrate the ways of our Lord by living righteously according to the Word of God. Let us be a *doer* of the word and not a *hearer* only (James 1:22).

Like our Father God heard the voice of His children, do not ignore the voice of any child or youth in the church. As we search our hearts, let us see beyond what we can see in reaching our children with love and compassion like Jesus did for us. Jesus loves the little children.

Matthew 18:2-5 - *"And Jesus called a little child unto him, and set him in the midst of them and said,* **Verily I say unto you, Except ye be converted, and become as little children, ye shall not enter into the kingdom of heaven. Whosoever therefore shall humble himself as this little child, the same is greatest in the kingdom** *of heaven and whoso shall receive one such little child in my name receiveth me."*

Matthew 18:10-11 – "*Take heed that ye despise not one of these little ones; for I say unto you, that in heaven their angels do always behold the face of my Father which is in heaven. For the Son of man is come to save that which was lost.*"

Jesus tells us where He stands concerning the little children: receive Him and we will have received all that He believed (Mark 9:37). We need to reach beyond what we can see in the life of a child; we are our brother's keeper. Reaching, sharing, and loving God's little ones is a great reward.

STOP, LOOK, AND LISTEN to a *Voice to Be Heard* from our youth in the 21st century. Remember kids are people too. Let's make a difference in the life of a child today for the generation of tomorrow.

Never allow our circumstances to stop us from hearing the cries of our kids in their time of need. What we teach and show our youth is reflected in their actions and character just as a mirror reflects an image. How are you developing today's youth to become tomorrow's leaders? What reflection are they seeing?

# Part II

# DEVELOPING YOUR

# YOUTH MINISTRY

- DEVELOPING YOUTH FOR THE MINISTRY
- THE BURDEN WE CARRY IS NOT OUR OWN
- DEVELOPING A PRAYER STRATEGY FOR YOUR YOUTH
- DECISION-MAKING
- DEVELOPING SPIRITUAL MENTORS FOR YOUR YOUTH
- MENTOR MINISTRY
- CHILDREN'S MINISTRY
- TEEN'S MINISTRY
- ABOUT STRAIGHT TALK
- JUNIOR STRAIGHT TALK
- TEEN'S STRAIGHT TALK
- TEENS REACHING TEENS

# Developing Your

# Youth Ministry

### Developing Youth for the Ministry

Developing youth for ministry takes prayer and discernment. Just because people are part of the church doesn't make them reliable. We must FOCUS on identifying youth who have leadership qualities and train them in the ways of the Lord. They will then help you discover and develop the skills and abilities of other youth. When God reveals our future leaders, we shouldn't hesitate to use them or delay preparing these individuals for service, or we could hinder the calling of their lives. Remember, many are called but few are chosen (Matthew 22:14). Not everyone can be a leader, but everyone can lead by example, playing a part in edifying the Body of Christ.

Impress upon those we choose as leaders the fact that they will have a great responsibility. Explain that they must realize the importance of their position and conduct themselves accordingly. While man may get distracted by the outward appearance, God looks at the heart. It is important for our leaders to maintain a

Godly attitude as well as appearance at all times because we never know who is watching. They should not be a pleaser of man, but a seeker of God.

We must encourage our youth to take a step of faith and believe that they are the ones who God has chosen to reach the world with the Gospel of our Lord and Savior Jesus Christ. Remember, God raises up special leaders and He gives us the responsibility to encourage, lead, and guide them in becoming who they are meant to be - *great leaders*.

All young people are special in their own way. Developing youth leaders is very critical; and we must establish a foundation for our youth groups to build upon. This foundation can make a difference in the Body of Christ.

In the youth group, develop a communication line that would allow them access to senior leaders and board members of the church. When all leaders live by example, the youth will desire to live the same way. This can help them when they are faced with challenges and tough decisions, and motivate them to do the Father's will and not be on their own agenda. When we teach them the principles, they will follow them without fail.

God's word says that without holiness no man shall see God (Hebrews 12:14). To love them is to show them, and to show them is to love them. The right way to live is a holy lifestyle. When we have the right agenda to live by, and they see it in the lives of their leaders, they will be able to recognize the Will of God in their own lives.

Developing the youth for the different ministries in our churches will help them to become future leaders, and will launch them into the next level of their life journey. When we develop these young people in the right way, they will be equipped to triumph over the evil one and to reach their peers. They will then be able to reproduce after their own kind.

What better way to reach the youth of tomorrow than by equipping, training, and developing the youth of today to become the future leaders that God called them to be.

The Word of God says train up a child (Proverbs 22:6). This generation of youth already has boldness. We must build upon that confidence and ensure they know that they can make a difference in this world by taking a stand for Christ.

# The Burden We Carry

# is Not Our Own

*"Oh, what peace we often forfeit. Oh, what needless pain we bear. All because we do not carry everything to God in prayer."*[1] Do these words mean anything to you? Are you carrying any burdens that do not belong to you? When the Body of Christ stops giving the enemy a foothold over our lives, we will see the Move of God in our churches. Most of our young people are faced with carrying the burden of raising their siblings and sometimes running the household while parents work. This is not the responsibility of any child who did not ask to be brought into this world, but it is the parents' and guardians' responsibility.

How many times have we seen children being forced to raise other children? This is not their problem. Parents often blame economic hardship for the reason they depend on older children to care for the younger ones. Well, the burden that parents and

---

[1]   "What a Friend We Have in Jesus" Poem (Joseph M. Scriven, 1855)

guardians put on youth today is totally ungodly. This is not a responsibility for our youth. They have enough on their plates to deal with. Some of them are already carrying the burden of raising a child of their own because of past misjudgments, so they really don't need the added responsibility of their parents' circumstances.

This behavior will only cause our youth to become unresponsive or rebellious. As parents and guardians, we will be held accountable for our actions and decisions in raising our children. We are to lead by example in raising an army of soldiers that will be bold for the Kingdom of God. We should not criticize our children for *everything* they say or do, and speak unkind things into their spirits. We often hold them to a standard that, at times, we ourselves cannot seem to meet. We must remember that these are children who are still learning and growing; and some of what they *do know* is coming from us. When our young people do (in our estimation) fail, we often punish them by withholding the very things that they need: contact with the people of God. We keep them from going to church and youth activities, which does more harm than good.[2]

Some of our youth are subjected to statements from parents and guardians like: *You will not amount to anything? You are a bum, you are stupid and lazy.* Or: *You are just like your daddy, good for nothing.* God is in control and is watching everything that is said

---

[2]    "Community involvement asset was related to youth decisions to not participate in a number of risk-taking behaviors, suggesting that engaging young people in volunteer service experiences in their communities holds potential as a protective factor in reducing certain adolescent health risk behaviors." (Rodine, Oman, Vesley, Aspy, Tolma, Marshall, Fluhr 2006)

and done in the life of a child. We will be held accountable for every idle word that comes out of our mouths (Matthew 12:36,37v). It's up to us, the men and women of God, to instill some positive memories into the lives of our youth. Show them that there is a place for them to come where they will be lifted up and not torn down; where they will be loved and not despised; where people are happy to see them, not angry that they are in the way. The Church receives broken youth of all ages all the time. As church leaders, we owe these broken vessels our commitment and our love.

Yes, we will face challenges, but we must rebuild their confidence, restore their faith, and refill their hearts with the Love of God. We must teach them to respect themselves and others, and have confidence and boldness to achieve and fulfill the purpose, plan, and destiny that God has for their lives. Teach them that the plan God has for their lives will come to pass, if only they will believe and trust in Him. As youth leaders, we must speak life into the lives of our youth and declare that they allow the Lord to use them for His purpose and His Glory.

The Word of God says it is better to give than to receive (Acts 20:35). Let us give until the job gets done or until our youth walk into the destiny that God has predestine before the foundation of the world.

Let's focus on how to win these youth back with the Word of God. When we are spiritually connected with God, then we can give back that which was given to us. We are our brother's keeper; cast all of our cares onto the Lord. Let's be real in the 21st century. Let go of your mess and let God do the rest.

If we follow the road map, the BIBLE (Basic Instructions Before Leaving Earth)—which is the Word of God—we can show God's people the truth in love. The Word of God can and will change, uproot, and pluck out anything that is not of Him. Let's speak with our youth and inform them that the unnecessary things that we make our burdens will take us out of the Will of God, or worse, kill us before our time.

Sometimes we take on other people's problems without thinking. God is the only one in control. Put your trust and confidence in our Lord to take control of your burden as well as other people's burdens too. 1 Peter 5:7 - *"Casting all your care upon him; for he careth for you."* James 5:16 - *"Confess your faults one to another, and pray one for another, that ye may be healed. The effectual fervent prayer of a righteous man availeth much."*

God's word says His yoke is easy and His burden is light (Matthew 11:30). God created everything, and everything we are is because of Him. If we only trust in Him to carry the burdens of His people He will give us rest and peace that surpasses all understanding (Philippians 4:7). We burn ourselves out when we allow the burdens of others to keep us from being all that God calls us to become. Help our youth understand that the decisions of their parents, guardians, and friends are *not* their burden to carry. They must learn to carry EVERYTHING to God in prayer.

When young people carry unnecessary burdens that they should take to God, they can end up depressed, frustrated, destructive, suicidal, and facing many more obstacles that are not intended for them at all. We must teach them to understand that the enemy will set them up for the fall. Satan's job is to destroy the mind, will, and emotions of those who are willing to walk upright in the admonition of the Lord. Satan is the enemy of the world. Let's equip our youth with the Word of God; and they will know how to fight the good fight of FAITH. The only way we can help our youth today is to instill in them that God wants it all, no matter how big it seems or how small it might be, just give it all to Him.

Releasing brings forth healing, and healing brings forth production and provision. We must be a living example to our youth of how positive things turn out when we put our trust in God's word; and that no matter what the problem might be, we believe that God will deliver us out of them all. Remind them that things may not always turn out like we want them to, but they can hold fast to: *"And we know all things work together for the good of them that love God, to them who are called according to His purpose"* (Romans 8:28).

Don't FOCUS on what doesn't belong to us; just know that *"The world is the Lord's and the fullness thereof and they that dwell within it"* (Psalm 24:1). Our FOCUS should be on Jesus. Please encourage your future youth leaders to take it to the Lord in prayer, because prayer is one of the most powerful and effective tools that God has ever given to mankind. Prayer has power. Let's use it before we lose it. Just remember, much prayer, much power; little prayer, little powers; no prayer, no power.

What a great assurance to know that the burden of others do not belong to us after all! Just be mindful of carrying everything (all) to the Lord, for He cares for us. And guess what? He and He alone died for us to be free from the bondage of this sinful world. We will be free from the bondage of this world by being obedient to God's word. 1 Peter 5:9 - *"Whom resist stedfast in the faith, knowing that the same afflictions are accomplished in your brethren that are in the world."*

Be real with yourselves, leaders, and be real with your youth, for God can and will do exceedingly and abundantly all that we can ask in the Name of Jesus. 1 Peter 5:6 - *"Humble yourselves therefore under the mighty hand of God, that he may exalt you in due time."* 1 Peter 5:5 - *"Likewise, ye younger, submit yourselves unto the elder. Yea, all* of you *be subject one to another, and be clothed with humility: for God resisteth the proud, and giveth grace to the humble."*

# Developing a Prayer

# Strategy for Our Youth

Many of our youth are afraid or embarrassed to open their mouths while praying during services. Just notice how so many of them are very loud in certain situations, for instance, in our youth rallies or youth sessions. We are unable to keep them quiet; they're so loud and crazy. But when it comes time to pray, notice that they go from loud to silent or you can barely hear the prayer that is being prayed.

Our youth are not shy at all but will try to fool you when it comes to prayer. Our job is to target the most outgoing or popular youth and encourage them to bring out the best in the other youths. Watch how God will use the very shy one to impact the world through the power of prayer. God will take the foolish things in this world to confound the wise (1 Corinthians 1:27).

We must nurture and encourage them when it comes to prayer. Make sure they never criticize or make fun of each other during prayer. This can cause a person to refrain from praying. You may have them start off slowly by just giving thanks for something or someone in their lives. As they get more comfortable sharing what is familiar to them, then you can watch how the Power of God moves upon them and their prayer life will get better. The more they pray, the stronger their prayer life becomes. Some of them may need a gentle push to open their mouths. Don't stop encouraging them. Let them know that God has placed a word in each of their hearts to speak.

This strategy in reaching our youth will make a big difference in the lives of other youths. What a great challenge to see powerful youths standing in the gap for each other in prayer. God is calling this generation to be bold and courageous (Joshua 1:9).

So, what are we asking the church leaders to do to impact this generation of future leaders? God is calling our church leaders to the front line to be bold with fire, to stand in these last and wicked days. He is calling for a radical generation of youth that will not compromise in the Body of Christ.

This is the time for prayer to be a part of our ministry like never before. If we look at our communities, schools, and churches, we can see the state of mind of the people who live and operate in them. If we don't get serious about our prayer life in the Body of Christ, how can we expect our youth to have a prayer life? Many youth cannot begin to achieve their greatest potential in life until they have begun a daily prayer life.

Ask the youth if they have a prayer request and allow them to receive prayer. Then ask them to pray for the group and other leaders. Remember, even the smallest prayer is heard in heaven, so continue to encourage and empower the youth by the power of the Holy Spirit in Jesus Christ our Lord.

Once, your youth group members seem comfortable in prayer, put into place a prayer strategy that will help them pray for one another. Allow them to have youth prayer breakfasts and prayer services, giving every youth the opportunity to lead prayer in the youth services and programs.

God is calling His people: every man, woman, boy, and girl to the front line to be bold and full of fire to stand in these last days. The call is for a radical generation that has known no compromise in His body. Now is the time for our youth to fight the good fight of FAITH by crying aloud in their prayers in Jesus' name and watch the Move of God.

Remember, as youth leaders, we must not take for granted the power of prayer ourselves. We must continue to develop a prayer strategy even for each leader to use as well as our youth. When we search the Word of God, it shows us how the power of prayer worked for the men of old. Prayer shut up heaven and there was no rain (1 Kings 8:35). Prayer stopped time. Joshua 10:13 – *"And the sun stood still, and the moon stayed, until the people had avenged themselves upon their enemies. Is not this written in the book of Jasher? So the sun stood still in the midst of heaven, and hasted not to go down about a whole day."* Prayer produced water from a rock (Exodus 17:6). Prayer protected the children of Israel, and delivered the three Hebrew boys from the fire (Daniel 3:26-27) and much, much more.

Get into the Word and prove your point by the Word of God. The Word of God will never be wrong. When you follow it, the truth will go forth with power. Always have an ear to hear the Word of God through prayer. Yes, a prayer life can change any situation if you believe.

# Decision-Making

Always open youth group meetings in prayer, especially when making decisions. I noticed that forming a circle with all participants involved is a great way to start the youth meeting. Involve all your youth in corporate prayer. Make sure to keep the seating in a circle format so everyone can have eye-to-eye contact with each other. The communication factor is very important in any group setting. You must stress how important it is that everyone is on one accord, respecting one another's opinion to make decision-making become a reality.

Write the vision and make a plan. Young people love visuals. Make sure to have an agenda on hand to provide to all the youth who will be part of this decision-making group. The first order of business is to vote in officers for the youth group. Make sure they are responsible and hold them accountable to the office they will hold.

Remember, it is wise to have the youth come up with the guidelines, procedures, rules, and regulations for the entire Youth Department to abide by. There should also be some consequences if they violate the rules. No excuses should be accepted for breaking the rules and regulations. Be sure that a list is posted for everyone to see. The youth helped to make the rules so they should be responsible for enforcing the rules.

When the youth leaders have been established, train them and see how fast the youth group will grow. Let's not be weary in doing well. Take one step at a time in equipping and teaching our future leaders. Please don't forget that they are young and have great ideals. They are eager to have a chance, if we will only allow them. Decision-making is important because the youth feel like they are part of a great vision that God has given the church. When the youth feel shut out of the church, your church will die. What do I mean? No youth, no future, and no church to carry on what God has commanded us to do.

Decision-making can be a lot of fun, but we must also take it seriously because we are setting a standard for all to follow. We make decisions everyday: some great, some small. God has given us a free will to receive or reject the plan for our lives. The choice is ours (yours). The right choice is the right way, which is The Way, Jesus Christ our Lord (John 14:6).

# Developing Spiritual Mentors for Your Youth

One way we can help our youth is to provide spiritual mentors for them. What is a spiritual mentor? A spiritual mentor is someone who is in right standing with God, who does not mind mentoring, witnessing, and encouraging young people. They must be led by the Spirit of God, and their heart must be pure. Mentors will impart values, the Word of God, and live by example with the lifestyle of holiness. It is not something to be taken lightly. It requires a true commitment to our youth to become a spiritual mentor. We are needed much more than we may realize. Our youth are looking, searching for direction and it's up to strong spiritual leaders to provide what they need on a consistent basis.

Too many times we begin programs for our youth, only to have them dwindle after a month or two, if that long. Our youth are facing some long term problems and they need some long term solutions, not band-aid fixes to gaping wounds. The challenges they face are urgent in nature; and they need immediate attention from those willing and prepared to stay the course and see them through until they become the self-confident, God-reliant spiritual leaders that God is calling them to be.

Jesus is our prime example of being a mentor to all who will receive His word. Jesus' ministry was one in which He guided, educated, and equipped, all the while mentoring, those who followed Him.

Our main duty is to be a witness for the world to see, while we glorify our Father in heaven. Mentoring youth is a very important task that should be undertaken after serious prayer and consideration. The Word of God tells us to know them that labor among you (1 Thessalonians 5:12). In other words not everybody has the ability to work with your youth. They must be tried and tested.

Our concern should be to know all we can about individuals willing to work with youth. Our youth watch and hear everything that we do and say. They are waiting for an opportunity to see if we are what we preach and waiting for us to teach them concerning the Word of God. Trust me, our body language and our appearance play an important part in how our youth react to us. Young people can spot a fake a mile away. They have a gift of knowing who is real with them or who is just full of lies and deceitfulness. The beauty of that is, they have no problem calling you out and their methods are not always tactful, but the truth is the truth, even if you don't like the delivery.

Our job as youth leaders is to weed out the nay-sayers and get leaders who are faithful to God's Word, the church, and the youth. Be sure to check the character of those individuals who claim they have been sent to mentor the youth. We don't want just anybody trying to impart in the lives of our youth. We need those who have been tried and tested and found faithful in the eyes of God and man (Psalm 26:2).

Please know that a mentor must be in good standing with the Body of Christ. Most of all, he or she must pay their tithes and offerings, attend church and Bible study on a regular basis, and be willing to go the extra mile if they have to for any youth they are mentoring. They must be willing to impart the wisdom, principles, Word, and the truth about life in general. They should continue to check on the status of their youth's school progress and activities, and their spiritual growth in the Body of God.

We must encourage our youth to achieve in every area of their life's journey and even beyond what they can imagine. Mentors must help them in time of trouble and need, assure them that God loves them no matter what situations they are faced with, and that prayer is the answer above all else. When we lead by example, our youth will follow. What we put in them will come out. It is important to pour in holiness. Believe me; holiness will come out of them. However, if we pour in garbage, *guess what*, garbage will definitely come out of them. Teach them that what they take in as a child of God is important to whom or what they will become.

Mentors are positive people who desire to give back what was imparted in their lives. They are givers and not takers, and they want the best for any young person's life. Mentors seek wise judgment through the Word of God, and will come boldly and confidently with a word of wisdom for one who is learning and hearing the truth.

Mentors are a great investment in the Body of Christ. For every youth to have someone who is willing to give up their time, talent, and treasure to help impact the life of a child is a great benefit to any church. A mentor does not want anything in return for what they are doing in the life of a child in need. Mentors know that their treasures are stored up in heaven (Matthew 6:20).

This person must be dedicated to at least **one full year** of mentoring a child, without any excuses or complaints that the child is bad or out of control. The mentor must help them in every area to learn how to become obedient to God and those who rule over them. They must complete a follow-up procedure with each child by showing that someone in the Body of Christ really loves them and is concerned about what really concerns them in this society of chaos.

Please make sure all mentors are fully aware of the commitment to the child they are mentoring and hold on to the word they release to each of them. Make sure they understand that the one full year commitment is important to every youth that puts their trust in their mentors to finish the task before each of them and don't be like the hypocrites in Matthew 6:1-4.

Every mentor needs to sign a commitment letter to show our youth the dedication of each mentor that will become a part of their faith-walk journey. The parents and the youth who have a mentor in their lives must also be willing to sign a commitment letter. This is considered a covenant agreement made between them and their mentor.

Once someone accepts the responsibility to become a youth mentor, they are telling that young person that they have become a part of their life now. Don't take being a mentor out of context. It's not just buying gifts for the child, but it's about imparting the gift of God and bringing out the very best part of them that may be lying dormant. Mentors must have the love and compassion of God, in Christ Jesus. They will not be able to reach their youth if this component in not implemented in their lives.

Living a holy lifestyle is an important factor in the Body of Christ because any little thing regarding your mentors can cause a youth to fall. So, as leaders, we must screen and know our mentors' characters no matter who they are in the Body of Christ. True workers for the Kingdom will not be offended regarding the character check. They also want someone who is truly going to make a worthwhile investment in our youth. A mentor is someone who is faithful and truthful to the church they are attending. His or her character speaks for itself in a positive way and is not questionable. They live by example according to the Word of God.

Rules and regulations are also important in selecting youth mentors. If someone cannot follow the rules of the church or the leadership of the pastor, then they may not be the right person to be a mentor. God's Word says obedience is better than sacrifices. 1 Samuel 15:21 – *"And Samuel said, Hath the LORD as great delight in burnt offerings and sacrifices, as in obeying the voice of the LORD? Behold, to obey is better than sacrifice, and to hearken than the fat of rams."* Remember, all the sacrifices we make in the world are nothing to God unless obedience is in front of it. If your mentors walk according to the Word and Will of God, then you have a winner.

Disappointment has played a big part in our youths' lives. Please don't start something you cannot finish because this is a serious matter to every youth who will become a part of your ministry. How beautiful are the feet of those who will win souls for Christ's sake? (Romans 10:15)

Words of Encouragement: Every youth group that establishes a girls and boys mentor program in their church will see firsthand how important it is to have someone invest in their children's lives by just caring.[3]

The Word of God says be faithful over a little and He will make us rulers over much (Matthew 25:23). Our children and youth have been disappointed so many times in their lives that it has become hard for them to believe in anyone at home, school or the church. Mentors are to continue to do what is right by leading a life of holiness.

The impact and the importance we have on their lives will encourage them to be the best they can be and become. Will you become a mentor and help change a life forever? The Word of God says those who win souls are wise. Proverbs 11:30 - *The fruit of the righteous is a tree of life; and he that winneth souls is wise.*"

---

[3] "...Youth who value religion and participate in congregation's activities are less involved with risk behaviors, it is possible that at-risk youth, in particular, may alter some of their behaviors if they are associated with a caring environment that stresses avoidance, pro-social behaviors, positive role models, and healthy relationships (Sinha and Canaan, Gelles 2004).

# Mentor Ministry

Mentor Ministry Day is a day set aside to address the life changes and disappointments that are real to a child, and help them to see a brighter day through the eyes of our Lord and Savior Jesus Christ.

Mentor Ministry Day is the beginning of developing a program for the sole purpose of getting to know the leadership, congregation, volunteers, and the youth that attend your church. So many churches do not have a clue who all the youth are that attend their church, let alone know their names or where they have come from or where they live.

On Mentor Day all mentors and youths can come together to share, encourage, empower, and learn more about each other's journeys in life. Mentors can get together and have a fellowship time with food and Christian games, and speak face-to-face with the youth that they are beginning to mentor. Have a Mentor Day once a month or however often you prefer. The frequency will depend on the area within the church, the people, the community, the church leaders, and many other factors.

I encourage all mentors to develop a time of the week just to call and check up on their child. A mentor needs to at least speak with their child once a week to help them Biblically with everyday issues that they are facing at school, home, and church. A mentor needs to be concerned with a child/youth's grades in school and progress at home and in church.

Mentors need to get a report once a month on every young person that they are mentoring, whether it's from home, school or the church. Accountability is so important in the life of a true mentor or mentored child. Always be willing to be in contact with parents or guardians regarding the child's attitude and behavior, watching for any signs of a problem with your child/youth.

A mentor must always be willing to encourage, speak the truth in love, and lead their child/youth to the Word of God in everyday trials and tribulations. We ask that mentors continue to encourage them to do what is right no matter what consequences that youth may face at any given time in their walk with God.

All mentors are to be a positive role model for the youth and their churches, and be willing to live a holy lifestyle wherever they go and in whatever they do in their walk with God. By no means should any mentor try to become more than a parent or guardian to their child. We are here to encourage our youth to have a relationship of communication with their parents or guardians at all times, by using the example of a relationship with our heavenly Father, God.

What a great privilege to give back what has been given to you as a mentor and as a child of the King. Then they will be able to give back what was given to them: love and words of encouragement to finish the race to the end. Mark 13:13 - *"And ye shall be hated of all men for my name's sake: but he that shall endure unto the end, the same shall be saved."*

# Children's Ministry

The Children's Ministry is a way to minister the Word of God to each child so they can relate and understand in a fun and loving way. This ministry is designed to reach children between the ages of 2 and 7 years old. Divide these children into two groups: 2 to 4 year olds, and then 5 to 7 year olds. You can really be creative regarding the Children's Ministry. You can reach them through a Puppet Ministry, Bible stories that teach them about the heroes in the Bible and how they made a difference, written plays, Vacation Bible School or arts and crafts. Children get excited about the different things you can come up with to keep their attention.

Developing a Children's Puppet Ministry for the 2 to 4 year olds and a Good News Club will be a great tool to start off with. But don't stop there because we have some very smart children. Teach them the books of the Bible through a song and you'll be surprised how fast they learn them. Arts and crafts are other activities that children enjoy because giving their loved ones a special gift that they made is great for them to receive love and attention.

This part of the Youth Ministry is a challenge within itself. It takes a special kind of person who is willing to work with children this age. Please make sure to have people that love to be around young children and are willing to go an extra mile to reach them with the Love of God.

**Kids across the world can be reached with God's love.**

1 Corinthians 13:2 – "*And though I have the gift of prophecy, and understand all mysteries, and all knowledge; and though I have all faith, so that I could remove mountains, and have not charity, I am nothing.*"

If someone is not sure if the Children's Ministry is for them, you may suggest they find another ministry because a children's group is not for everybody. Whoever considers this ministry might need to stand still and allow God to direct their path. Patience, kindness, and tender-loving care are desperately needed for this generation. The Children's Ministry can be a great asset to any church family. What better way to start training them than while they are young and eager to try various things and be effective in what they learn.

Jesus speaks out regarding the children in Matthew 18: 1-10. We must become like little children to enter into the Kingdom of God. Matthew 19:14 - "*But Jesus said,* **Suffer little children, and forbid them not, to come unto me; for of such is the kingdom of heaven.**"

Kids have a mind of their own and their attention span is not very long. They start out doing one thing and then change their mind to do something else. We must know and understand that children are in a learning pattern and they have so much to absorb in such a short period of time.

We ask youth leaders and adults to set an example for this generation so that they can take over and reach the world with love and compassion with the knowledge we have instilled in them.

Man is the only creation that God made that will not let their children go. Let go and let God perform wonderful works in our children's lives. We have seen nothing yet! God is raising an army of youths that will impact this generation with the Gospel of Jesus Christ our Lord.

Rise up and walk mighty warriors, soldiers in the Army of the Lord! It's time to take a stand; it is time to fight the good fight of FAITH!

# Teen Ministry

In today's society it is important to tell our teens to be followers of Christ and not man. The majority of our teens will not set a standard in their lives to follow Christ because most of them want to be accepted by their peers, no matter what the price.

Being a teen in this day and age is a great challenge for young people. If you ask me, they love to "buck" authority. They seem to have their own opinion regarding everything and are eager to become something they are not just to be accepted in the most popular groups.

When meeting with a group of young people, the majority of the teens tend to gravitate to the strong-willed person. This particular teen becomes the spokesperson for the entire group. This can become a great problem if this teen is a problem child. We must watch our teens. If we notice a change in their behavior, this is a concern. We must find out who they are hanging around with or what they have been exposed to. Many times teens can get involved in alcohol, drugs, cigarettes, sex, and much more.

As parents, guardians, youth leaders, pastors, teachers, and mentors, we are to do exactly what the Word of God tells us to do in equipping our youth to become witnesses for Christ. God commanded His children to: "***Go ye therefore, and teach all nations, baptizing them in the name of the Father, and of th4e Son, and of the Holy Ghost: Teaching them to observe all things whatsoever I have commanded you: and, lo, I am with you always, even unto the end of the world.*** *Amen*" (Matthew 28:19-20).

The Teen Ministry is our chance to reach them before we lose them.

# About Straight Talk

Straight Talk is a youth group geared toward junior teens and teens where they can:

- Develop good relationships with other youth
- Learn unconditional Love and respect for others
- Understand Biblical discipline and correction
- Develop trust and confidence in the Word of God
- Establish a relationship/trust with leaders and volunteers
- Speak the truth in Love
- Have a way to express hurt and pain caused by others
- Have *A Voice to Be Heard*
- Cry out as troubled youth

# A STATEMENT TO THE PARENTS ABOUT STRAIGHT TALK

In Straight Talk, we give every youth the right to share their personal information in the group without their parents. We discourage the sharing of other people's issues with anyone outside the group. Trust is the foundation for relationships. We are a bridge to you. We know that children find it difficult to communicate with their parents about sensitive issues. We promise to communicate all life-threatening or dangerous issues to you directly, in confidence.

A Straight Talk agreement is an agreement made between the youth of the Church and the Youth Ministry Leadership Team along with their parents, guardians, and volunteers.

# EXAMPLE STRAIGHT TALK AGREEMENT

I _____ (youth's name) will be a participant in a Straight Talk session once a week in our Youth Ministry Group to help me better understand the things that are happening in society, my life, and in the church I am attending. I will have the opportunity to fellowship with other teens/junior teens in our Straight Talk sessions where I will learn how to cope with the issues I am faced with daily.

As a participant in Straight Talk sessions with the other teens/junior teens and Youth Leaders, I will commit to keeping whatever is released in Straight Talk sessions private and between us, unless it is a life or death situation. Then, and only then, will any issue be addressed to the senior pastor and parents or guardians of the youth involved. I understand that I am trusted not to spread anything that I've heard through our Straight Talk experience because it is important that the confidence of the group be kept in a way where no one will feel or think that their trust has been broken.

I understand that this agreement will be signed by our Youth Leaders who are persons of integrity, faithfulness, and who are trust-worthy to the Youth Ministry. I understand that this agreement is a covenant between all parties who are involved in teaching, equipping, and helping to support me in my walk of life.

*To leadership and volunteers:* By signing this agreement you are committing to **one full calendar year** in this ministry.

Signatures: _____ Date: _____
Youth Leader

_____ Date: _____
Parent or Guardian

_____ Date: _____
Volunteer

# Junior Straight Talk

We usually have a lot of programs for this age group to participate in so they can remain busy. But this is the season and time for a change where our youth can be part of a great Move of God. It is written: out of the mouth of babes (Psalm 8:2). Just listen. By doing this you can form programs that will meet the needs of your juniors and develop future teen leaders and great youth speakers.

Junior Straight Talk is geared to help children between the ages of 8 and 11 years old. Just like the Teen Ministry's Straight Talk, this age group's Straight Talk is greatly needed. They need someone to minister to their needs and understand the concerns within their hearts. Our youth must be able to know and believe that there are people sent from God to help them with whatever situations that might occur in their lives.

Kids of this age are more visual. Junior Straight Talk is a little different atmosphere than the Teen Ministry's. In this group, they are asked to write down questions that are on their minds and in their hearts. They learn Christian raps and Bible scriptures. I noticed that open discussion is great for them to express themselves. They love being in a small group setting with boys and girls acting out Bible characters that they have learned throughout the year. Try it as a contestant-like game. These methods allow them to challenge their opponents in a group setting. *"And the winner is…"* Believe me, they love to win.

Also, the youth leaders must be very creative with this group. They will ask a thousand and one questions. *"Why does this have to be done this way?"* This generation wants a change in life. What it took to keep us in church will not be the same for them. This generation is starving for more and more. What are you going to feed them? Put garbage in and garbage comes out. Put holiness in and holiness comes out. Choose wisely.

Let's be mindful that we must live by example and lead this generation to the next dimension. We must be able to become their spiritual moms and dads. This is a big concern for this generation because there is a lack in the majority of their homes: no fathers or mothers. Many of them are being raised by grandparents or great-grandparents. What a mess we have allowed to take place in our homes. Churches must take the lead and teach God's people the right way to be Godly parents.

Get ready for the great Move of God, for it's coming faster than you can see. Romans 12:2 – *"Be ye transformed by the renewing of your mind."* Don't wait; get a move on this great explosion for these 21st century youths. Developing a sound program is essential for this generation. When youth feel needed and wanted in their lives, they will get the confidence and the boldness to take a step of FAITH and make things happen for themselves.

We must FOCUS on the things that concern them and listen to what they are saying, for if it's important to them, let it be important to us also. Be honest with them, and allow them to do the same as they speak about their needs. Make them feel and know that they are special in God's eyesight and ours also. Junior Straight Talk is a great benefit for any youth group.

# Teen Straight Talk

As leaders and teachers at the House of Prayer, we believe it's a God-given assignment to equip, edify, encourage, and develop our youth ministry. It's vital that our youth be trained in the Word of God, "*Endeavoring to keep the unity of the Spirit in the bond of peace*" (Ephesians 4:3). Part of that responsibility is dealing with and sharing the natural part of life. Being able to communicate real issues in a non-threatening, non-judgmental, Biblical atmosphere where love is demonstrated (Romans 5:8) has proven to help our children avoid pitfalls.

If we could develop this concept in all churches, we would see an awesome change in the youth groups. Please hear the voice of our youth. Motivate them by giving personal testimonies. How can we be effective in reaching our youth if we have never been through anything?

Straight Talk is a ministry implemented for the instruction and development of youth throughout the world. If Straight Talk is presented correctly, this can be a vital part of the Youth Ministry Department. Screen all leaders and volunteers. Everybody cannot work with young people. They must have a love for youth and a respect for their privacy. We discourage the sharing of any youth issues outside the group.

If ever any pastor, leader, volunteer or parent breaks the confidence of any one of their youth, it will take a long time for them to be able to trust the church leaders again. We must be so mindful of the trust factor in our churches today. So many people have been hurt by "church folks" that they believe we are all alike. How many of us are willing to go the extra mile in building a relationship of truth and trust?

# Teens Reaching Teens

What a great command to do the will of the Lord. If we train them and teach them to live according to the Word of God, how great it will be to have our youth and teens ministering to each other. They need to know that they can make a wonderful difference in the life of a child. The world will teach our teens how to walk in disobedience everyday and miss knowing *whose* they are in Christ Jesus. What a difference a day will make in teaching and equipping this generation that the world considers to be lost.

When we as parents, guardians, pastors, youth leaders, and mentors make a stand and teach and equip these future leaders, then God will pour out His Spirit among all flesh (Joel 2:28). Then, and only then, will we see a change in our youth.

Today, teens can reach others teens if we just allow them to be themselves. We must not focus on the outward appearance but on the heart (1 Samuel 16:7). God has given them a unique way of communicating to each other's needs. A teen in need will always find another teen to feed from. If our teens are fed right, you can expect that they will follow us in teaching other teens the right way. There is an old saying: Do as I say and not as I do. *Wrong.* These teens today will not do as you say but will definitely do as you do. The confidence and boldness that you impart in the life of a teen will go far as one can see.

Teens that reach other teens are those who are trained, chosen, and not ashamed of the Gospel of Jesus. They indeed have *A Voice to Be Heard*. What a great reward in knowing or seeing our teens give back what was given to them in their journey of life. Youth will see that sowing a seed into the life of another can spread throughout the world. Just try it. If we would only allow the seed that we plant to be watered by our teens, we will know without a shadow of a doubt that God will give the increase.

Don't take for granted that a problem teen cannot be reached. If God kept us, He can keep anyone. We must look into our own lives and ask God to show us how to reach these teens. Seeing with a spiritual eye will bring us back into reality. STOP, LOOK, and LISTEN before we open our mouths. We should be speaking from the Heart of God and not man. "*With loving-kindness have I drawn thee*" (Jeremiah 31:3). Now that's a word! Teens can be reached by other teens. Try it; you will like it. Change can make a difference. Without it, your teen group will die.

# Part III

# WHERE IS THE CHURCH?

- WHERE IS THE CHURCH
- WHAT ROLE DOES THE CHURCH PLAY IN THE 21ST CENTURY?
- A VOICE TO BE HEARD
- WHAT ARE TEENS FACED WITH TODAY?
- YOUTH PEER PRESSURE
- HEARING (LISTENING TO) THE WRONG VOICE
- A CRY OUT FOR TROUBLED TEENS
- DOES ANYONE CARE ABOUT ME?
- WHO REALLY LOVES ME?
- HELP IN THE TIME OF TROUBLE
- DO YOU KNOW WHO YOU ARE?
- DO YOU KNOW HIM?
- A WAY OUT
- WHO WILL PRAY FOR ME?
- INTERCESSORY PRAYER FOR TEENS
- A CHANCE TO BE FORGIVEN
- A COVENANT LETTER WITH TEENS, VOLUNTEERS, AND STAFF LEADERS

# Where Is The Church?

What a peculiar question to ask: *Where is the Church?* When talking about developing an effective youth ministry, the church should be at the forefront of the conversation; but, sometimes what is really needed from the church is not always available. The church can get stuck within the four walls of a building and at times be pleasers rather than fishers of men (Mark 1:17). We have lost all sense of who we really are supposed to be in the Body of Christ.

The Church may have lost the knowledge of who she was meant to be. When one cannot tell the difference between the church and the world, the church is truly in trouble. We have reached a place where we have convinced ourselves that the work of the Lord can be done entirely within the walls of our church. How wrong the Body of Christ is, for God has given all believers a commandment to go and tell the world (Matthew 28:19-20). We fail to come out from beyond the walls that we have built to fulfill our own selfish desires.

Our priorities have become as the worlds: obtaining things. We have put our focus on fancy buildings, big houses, and cars –

everything, except winning souls for Christ. Our sense of being led by the Spirit has been lost trying to obtain the wealth of the world. Where is our FOCUS concerning the Word of God, through Jesus Christ our Lord? We continue, in the 21st century, to deceive ourselves, thinking we are better than those who are of the world when we are not different than they.

At times, the Church has hidden behaviors, hiding behind masks of fear, deceit, and greed, while destruction and chaos has filled this world. We are supposed to live *in* and not *of* this world. It is written in the Word of God: "*Love not the world, neither the things that are in the world. If any man loves the world, the love of the Father is not in him*" (1 John 2:15). The Church has become lovers of their own souls, and having a lustful desire for accomplishing the things of the world, instead of winning souls for Christ as commanded.

Where, oh where, is the Church of the Body of Christ? **We cannot continue to fail our youth.** We must teach and preach the living Gospel of Jesus Christ to a dying world. We have to come out from behind the four walls and reach those who are not following Christ. It is up to the Church to make a difference in the lives of people. We cannot keep on seeking fame and glory, stroking our own egos with program after program, rewarding ourselves for what – ministering to each other? We must let a dying world know about a risen Savior who can cleanse them from their sins and welcome them into an eternal home with Him.

It is our duty to get out of our comfort zones, from behind our church walls, and open the church doors to go out into streets, highways, and byways to spread the Gospel of the saving power of Jesus Christ. The Church needs to be awakened by Almighty God, by His Spirit, so that the believers - the saints, the Body of Christ - can take a stand and become who God has intended them to become: the head and not the tail (Deuteronomy 28:13), above and not beneath. We are to be a light in time of darkness, shining through a lost and perverted generation of vipers where sin has taken over like there is no hope in the land.

*Where is the Church?* She must arise from a place of darkness and sin and come back into the light where we are to take charge once again and become the light of the world.

*Where is the Church?* She must stand under persecution and distress, spreading and sharing the Love of God through Christ Jesus, our Lord.

*Where is the Church?* She must take her rightful place and prepare to take over a lost generation of unbelievers by being all that God has commanded her to be.

*Where is the Church?* She must pray without ceasing in the Body of Christ for all who are lost.

*Where is the Church?* She must stand on the promises (and not just *sit* on the premises) that God has already given to our forefathers.

*Where is the Church?* She must be led by the Spirit of God to fulfill the greatest commission ever given to man from God our

Father. We are that Church that will go and teach and love and be a help in time of trouble to as many as receive the Lord.

*Where is the Church?* She must take her place back from society and live the resurrected life that God has empowered her to live by the cleansing of His word.

Who *is the Church?* It is each individual who confesses that Jesus is Lord and believes in their hearts that God raised Him from out of the grave with all power and authority given to those who freely receive Him as their Savior.

The question to every believer is: If the Church is in us, where, oh where, have we been concerning our youth in this 21st century generation? The Church *must* and *will* train and equip through the knowledge and power of Jesus Christ. No longer will anyone say *Where is the Church?* She has to be in position, ready and willing to fight the good fight of FAITH and impact and encourage this world with the Gospel of Jesus Christ our Lord.

As a youth leader you must be ready to say: Here is the 21st century church, ready to stand for righteousness according to the Word of God, and to love one another as Christ our Lord has loved us, willing to feed God's sheep with the truth until Jesus Christ our Lord's return to take His bride home, the Church.

When someone asks, "*Where is the Church?*" tell them: On the front line with prayer and supplication, making our request made known unto the Father who created heaven and earth for His called and chosen children of this 21st century.

# What Role Does the Church Play in the 21st Century?

*What part does the Church play?* I tell you, it is a very important part. God gave us a command to reach the world with the Gospel of Jesus Christ our Lord. If the Church sits down and does not go into all nations, we will not continue to have *A Voice* (needing) *to Be Heard.* Everything we need to reach the world is in the Word of God, so we just need to use the tools God has given us to win souls for Christ.

The Church will be judged first for her lack of involvement. Staying behind the four walls of a building does not put us in the Will of God. We must have the Father's Heart and His will so none can perish. What can we do as Christians (Christ-like)? Get up, repent, and put on the whole Armor of God so that we can reach this dying world with the Gospel of our Lord and Savior, Jesus Christ.

We, the Church, have so much to do in a short period of time, that we do not have any time to criticize anyone else's ministry.

The Word of God will judge us all, whether it is good or bad. Only what we do for God will last. Isaiah 40:8 - "*The grass withereth, the flower fadeth: but the word of our God shall stand for ever.*"

Let's take another look at some of the many things that can be implemented into our churches. Don't be afraid of making changes. Without change and a vision, the ministry will die.

**Reach, Build, and Trust are our three key words.**

**BUILD**. It only takes a few young people to make a difference. Train them so we can get an army for the Lord. Young people will evangelize without knowing it. Teens reaching teens works.

**REACH**. Open up a line of communication with the youth. Allow them to voice their opinions. Then be honest with them. Let them know that changes are important. Let me give you a little advice leaders and volunteers: learn how to talk *to* them and not *at* them.

**TRUST**. It is important to establish and build good relationships with our youth. They will trust us when we are ourselves with them. Learning how to respect them will help them respect others.

Set a standard of teaching and direction. God's word says:

Hosea 4:6a - "*My people are destroyed for lack of knowledge.*"

Proverbs 29:18a - "*Where there is no vision, the people perish.*"

Proverbs 3:5-6 - *"Trust in the Lord with all thine heart; and lean not unto thine own understanding. In all thy ways acknowledge him, and he shall direct thy paths."*

Apply these scriptures in setting up youth groups in the 21st century. It takes the entire community to raise a child. The role of the church can be a very instrumental factor. What do I mean? Well, in most of the churches today, the parents will usually send their children to church and not attend with them. This is one of the biggest problems churches are faced with when handling youth groups. Please, don't ever turn a child away because of lack of parental involvement. We must let it be known to the parents that we are not a baby-sitting service. We are here to impart the Word, Knowledge, and Wisdom of our Lord and Savior, in the life of their child.

Through the following activities, we can reach our youth. I have discussed some of these in detail previously. Develop your own activities and watch your youth flourish.

- **Straight Talk**
- **Teen Basic Training**
- **Reward Program**
- **Prayer Partner**
- **VBS (Vacation Bible School)**
- **Children Discipleship and Development Programs**
- **Community Day (An Out Reach to your Community)**
- **Youth Service every Fifth Sunday (or whatever you decide)**
- **Christian Camps (Kids Across America)**
- **Boys Mentor's Day**
- **Girls Mentor's Day**
- **Sunday School**

- **Youth meeting once or twice a month**
- **Youth Evangelism Training (and going out on the street)**
- **Youth Praise Dancers Group**
- **Youth News Letter (Teen Reporters)**
- **Youth Choir/Praise & Worship Team**

Always take them back to the Word of God. This will help them to grow and depend on God's word. Many of them do not know how to use a BIBLE; show them how and make them responsible. A Teen Bible is a great asset in helping them to develop their walk with God. The Word is written in a manner that is easily understood by youth.

Remember, be an example of Christ for them to follow. The key is that we must live by example. Set a standard for your volunteers and youth leaders. Don't do anything you don't want them to do. Make sure the entire Youth Ministry Department signs a commitment letter. And don't forget to let your youth help with developing a procedure form regarding the rules and regulations. Most importantly, let your youth know without a doubt that they have *A Voice to Be Heard*.

## A Voice to be Heard – "What should the Church do for kids in the 21st Century?"

Here are some youths sharing their opinion regarding life in the 21st Century.

*Nice things, Love and Joy should be coming from the Church. God should take care of the world and take care of His people. The kids are to obey God whatever He says and obey their parents.*

**--Dennis Keyon Craig, Age 6**

*I believe the Church can reach out to as many teens as possible. The teens are the future and the Church needs to help in their training. The Church also needs to let the youth know that they have the adults to talk to. Let the youth know they are Loved and that they are also needed in the Church.*

**--Candace Brooks, Age 16**

*The Church can help teens by listening to them more. Often in the Church, teens are to be seen and not heard, and because of that they don't have any say so in the Church. The reason why is because they most likely judge us for our outer appearance and not our inner heart, or they believe we don't know what we are talking about, but the Word of God says that "the children shall lead them." Another way is to train the teens because out the month of babes... So train us and when we are trained then we can reach other teens with the Word of God, so that the devil cannot touch us. This is how the Church of the 21st century can help teens of the 21st century.*

**--Christopher Williams, Age 16**

*What the Church can do to help me in the 21st century is to talk more about life, because people think life is a joke and easy. It is not because when you grow up it is not going to be easy, let kids know more about the God we worship and some of the adults too.*

*--**Tyrone Cole, Age 12***

*How can the Church help the youth in the 21ˢᵗ century? Continue to pray for the youth, help them with their problems, have talks about their problems in how we will know how to solve their problems, have praying classes and also pray for the ones who needs prayer.*

*--**Helena Harrison, Age 12***

*What can help kids in the 21ˢᵗ century as well as the Church is to let people know if they follow God, bad things will not happen as much. But if you don't, hopefully God will forgive you for all the bad things that they have done. But you know I try to follow God and every time, I do something in sin, I try to keep my head up and you should too.*

*--**Chris Jones, Age 12***

*What a Church can do to help me in the 21ˢᵗ century is to talk more about life because people think life is easy but it is not because you think you can do things easy; then it starts to get hard because you have to pay bills and get to work on time. But if you just believe in God you know you can do all things through Christ that strengthen me and everything will be all right.*

*--**Tyrone Glover, Jr. Age 13***

*The Church can help the youth by continuing to have straight talk and allow young people to say what they think about what is going on in the 21ˢᵗ century like: drugs, sex, and gangs, etc. Because if all the youth in the world can have someone to talk to maybe there would not be so many diseases and deaths, only if a child can have someone who understands, what kids go through.*

*--**Keonna Harrison, Age 14***

*The Church can help the youth of the 21ˢᵗ century by showing them love, not the love that is shown for your favorite candy bar or the love that is shared between married couples, but the Churches need to show the children unconditional love and the love of Jesus Christ. This type of love was shared with me when I came to The House of Prayer for All Nations Ministries, and it helped me overcome many of the trials that were before me. This love lets you know that no matter what you go through or how you feel, you have someone that loves you.*

**--David Armster, Age 14**

*Number one: outside basketball, football, and smiling.*

**--Mark Dishman, Age 15**

*The Church can support the youth in the vision that God has set in them. We will need the Church to give us a respectable amount of time to better the youth music ministry and other ministries that shall include winning souls for Christ.*

**--Fountain Hendricks, Age 19**

# A Voice to be Heard

We have to put to the side the old saying that "kids are to be seen and not heard" and listen to the voices of our youth. They have *A Voice to Be Heard*. Let them have a voice in decision-making; it can change your life and theirs forever. Jesus wanted to hear from the children in Mark 10:14 – "*But when Jesus saw it, he was much displeased, and said unto them,* **Suffer the little children to come unto me, and forbid them not: for of such is the kingdom of God.**"

Hearing the voice of our youth is vital to developing a successful youth ministry. Youth know what they want and what they need. Our young people have a right to be heard and we *want* them to know they are *going* to be heard. But, at the same time, make sure to impress upon them that everything must be done according to God's Word, decently and in order. It's our responsibility to ensure that what we give to our youth lines up with the Word of God. Our first priority should be to follow God's Word.

As Christians, our duty—or command—is to do as the Word of God tells us to do, so we must be diligent in making sure our youth program is spiritual. We don't want to send mixed messages to our youth by saying one thing and doing another. In other words, we don't want to create a secular atmosphere during our ministry activities while, at the same time, trying to tell them what "thus said the Lord." We need the two to mirror each other. We want what we tell them and what they actually do to convey the same message.

Remember, all eyes are on us. Kids are always watching. They see us even when we don't see them. We must be very careful of our actions at all times. Something as trivial as how we say good morning to someone can have a negative impact on our youth. Our youth look to us to show them how to become followers of Christ. We have to do more than teach. We also have to lead. Don't just tell them, show your youth how to handle conflicts and disagreements, by going to your brother or sister in love. Matthew 5:23 - "*Therefore if thou bring thy gift to the altar, and there rememberest that thy brother hath ought against thee;* [24] *Leave there thy gift before the altar, and go thy way; first be reconciled to thy brother, and then come and offer thy gift.*"

Set a standard for your volunteers and your youth leaders. Not everyone can work with youth. It takes a lot of understanding, patience, and commitment to work with youth. The key is to live by example. Don't do anything you don't want them to do. The Greater Eye of God is on you too!

Jesus is a primary example for us to follow. He heard the voice of the children crying aloud. Parents, guardians, and leaders sometimes fail to hear the cries of the youth. No one knows the cry of a child better than a mother. When babies are born, parents hear several different cries: a cry when the child is wet, a cry when the child is hungry, and a cry when the child is sleepy. After the baby stage is over, and the child moves into the difficult years (when you really should hear them), the parents tend to lose the ear to hear the voice of their children. The cry of the youth is ringing loud throughout the world.

What happens when the cry of the children go unanswered? Pharaoh is a good example of what will happen when we don't listen to the voice of God's children crying out to be heard. Many plagues covered the land of Egypt as a result of ignoring the cry of the children. The same is happening today. We see in our youth the consequences of a voice not heard: DRUG/ALCOHOL ABUSE, LYING TONGUE, ANGER, STEALING, MURDER, **DISOBEDIENCE** just to name a few. The list goes on and on, all ending in tragedy. [4]

Mark 8:36 tells us, *"For what shall it profit a man, if he shall gain the whole world, and lose his own soul?"* Trying to keep a roof over your head and food on the table is very vital to living and unfortunately becomes more important than providing something that our youth really need....your time. Too many times youth are allowed to see or hear things that do not concern them. Our focus gets shifted and we sometimes put other things before God and fail to hear His voice on what the Word tells us about our children. Youth need love and discipline, nurturing and guidance, and patience and firmness.

Christian parents and spiritual leaders are greatly needed in our churches more than ever before. It is so important that the father *and* mother work together to raise their children. Youth leaders need to work with parents to monitor what youth read, watch,

---

[4]   Read Exodus beginning with Chapter 5

wear, and speak. It's up to us to hear the youth and respond to the need. God has given us His spirit to love unconditionally and to hear the voice of one who is crying aloud. When you FOCUS on the things that are above, God will give you all you need to help hear the voice of His children.

There will always be challenges when working with youth. Don't be discouraged. God did not call you into this ministry to fail. Sometimes the kids won't listen. Sometimes it will seem like you aren't making a difference. You may even encounter opposition from leadership, but keep going. Continue to get your strength from the Lord. Continue to ask for His guidance and keep seeking God's Will. Ephesians 5:17 – *Wherefore be ye not unwise, but understanding what the will of the Lord is.*"

# What are Teens Faced
# with Today?

The majority of our teens are faced with growing up before their time. Teens want to be grown, acting as if they have a married lifestyle. They are faced with deception, oppression, confusion, alcohol, drugs, sexual desires, low self-esteem, child abuse, and so much more. The pressures of this life and the lifestyle of their parents, church leaders, and peers are conflicting and confusing which causes youth to seek help in the wrong direction.

Everybody wants to belong to something, even if it's the wrong thing. Health clubs, book clubs, secret societies, gangs - that is our way of connecting with each other. The main principle we want to instill in our youth is to be connected to the Body of Christ. We want them to understand that the ultimate relationship is one with God. With Him there are no hidden fees, no risks, and no restrictions. The youth need to understand that when they belong to God's family, the rewards are instant and eternal. Their membership cannot be revoked or suspended if they don't follow all the rules to the letter. They need to understand that God is a forgiving God who will wipe away their sins and give them eternal membership.

As youth leaders, we must teach our young people that there are stages in life. You don't come out of the womb as an adult, like portrayed in the story: *The Curious Case of Benjamin Button.*[5] We cannot treat them just like the world does. *"If you think you're grown, then we'll treat you like you're grown."* They are still children, and we must treat them as such. That is the reason why there are so many secular laws on the books protecting children, because they cannot reason well enough to protect themselves. So many of our teens die before their time: mentally, spiritually, and physically because there are so few willing to step up and help our children. Society has tried to help, but there are only so many programs they can create, and if no one takes the children to them, how will they get the help they so desperately need? When will the Body of Christ take their rightful place and be responsible for reaching our teens—our future leaders? It really is up to us, the Body of Christ, to take the lead with our youth. Society will only teach them so much. We have to prepare our youth for a world that is waiting to devour them. 1 Peter 5:8 – *Be sober, be vigilant; because your adversary the devil, as a roaring lion, walketh about, seeking whom he may devour.*

Our youth are being bombarded on every side by the media, their peers, and society as a whole, with every kind of immoral thing you can imagine. Some of the things they see and hear are so disgusting that it is hard to understand how some of our youth are as stable as they are. Everybody is telling somebody about

---

5   "The Curious Case of Benjamin Button" Short Story (F. Scott Fitzgerald, 1921)

their body to anybody. We need to just STOP and see how the enemy has blinded us by having us focus on *stuff* instead of the struggle that our teens are really faced with today.

AWAKE Church, and arise with the power and authority that was given unto us by JESUS to aid us in reaching and teaching our youth with the truth. The Word of God says, "*Ye shall know the truth and it shall make you free, and whom the Son set free is free indeed*" (John 8:32).

What are youth faced with today? Not knowing the truth or what's real. They need to know that Jesus is for real. John 14:6 – "Jesus *saith unto him,* **I am the way, the truth, and the life: no man cometh unto the Father, but by me.**" We take for granted that youth know who God is, but they don't have a clue. If the truth be told, there are many adults who don't know who God is, so it's very critical to the future of our youth that they develop a deep relationship with God. We do not want our youth to be like the children of Israel, wandering through the wilderness for years before they reach the promise land that God has for them.

We must be real with this generation and they will be real with us. They are truly seeking the truth in this hour. So many of them are tired of the lifestyle and the behavior they are in. When we, as leaders are real to ourselves, we can be real with our youth. We must not make the mistake that youth don't understand or are not ready for the truth. They have more knowledge and intelligence than we give them credit for. Most of the knowledge they get comes from places other than the church and may not be very accurate. As youth leaders, we want to make sure they have the correct information when making decisions that could affect their lives. The truth is found in the Word of God; everything our youth need is in His word. They should know that life is so much more difficult without God's word which is a lamp unto our feet and a light unto our path (Psalm 119:105).

Many youth face life without having anyone to hear their voices. What does God value? God values His people. We should value what God values (Luke 12:7). Our teens are people too, so value what God values, and speak the truth in love.

# Youth Peer Pressure

Youth today are faced with peer pressures from everywhere in the world. Young people are always trying to become something they are not because society puts so many demands on them. Everywhere they look there are images of what they should be. Be skinny. Have long hair. Have short hair. Dress like this. Live in that kind of house. Talk like this. Listen to this kind of music. Dance like that. The list is endless, and almost everything they see and hear has a sexual overtone.

Wow! It has become so bad that many of our youth have developed negative attitudes towards parents, siblings, and anyone else who tries to tell them the truth in love. An identity crisis is gripping our youth in a frightening way. The generation of tomorrow needs help now. How do we help our youth when society has labeled them as being rebellious and out of control? Their "rebellion" could very well just be a cry to be heard, and the "out of control" character could be a matter of no discipline. Many of our young people are growing up without a father, leaving our young men with no positive male influence to show them how to become real men; and causing our young women to go from man to man, seeking the male nurturing they didn't get as little girls.

We need men of God to take their rightful place in the Body of Christ. Where, oh where, are the mighty men of valor?

First of all, let's take a closer look at the environment we have created where our youth feel comfortable. Youth are allowed to talk to parents about what they like and dislike in any manner that suits them at the time. We often ask who are the parents, them or us? A dysfunctional child or youth normally has a dysfunctional parent or parents. Most of our youth gravitate toward other youths who have strong wills and the ability to control others. This puts them in the hands of the enemy. It is our responsibility as youth leaders to do our best to keep them away from things that keeps them away from God.

The youth of this generation want to belong to something or someone. Peer pressure will cause them to do things that they don't even want to do like lying, stealing, bragging or alcohol and substance abuse, which leads to acting out angrily, becoming depressed, becoming sexually active, attempting or committing suicide, and much more that we may never know about.

Peer pressure can hit any house or church. It knows no name. How can we, as the Body of Christ, help our youth when we don't hear their cry for help? We must pay attention to the signs that they are displaying. Their body language is a key factor in reaching a teen that is under peer pressure.

Some red flags that will allow you to see that something is seriously wrong are: unrest, anxiety, disturbances, lack of interest or concentration, agitation of the mind, lack of communication, change in attitude, physical appearance, behavior, and change of language. If you notice any of these behaviors, get help *quickly*. Peer pressure can cause our youth to harm themselves or others without even understanding what happened.

It takes a village and a community to raise the youth of today. Pay attention. Don't allow the enemy to have you say "not my child," and ignore their cries. Have an open relationship with them; talk about everything. Understand that peer pressure is real. Watch and pray without ceasing. Remember, this is a Spiritual battle not a physical (fleshly) one. Ephesians 6:12 – "*For we wrestle not against flesh and blood, but against principalities, against powers, against the rulers of the darkness of this world, against spiritual wickedness in high places.*" Psalm 34:19 – "*Many* are *the afflictions of the righteous: but the Lord delivereth him out of them all.*"

# Hearing (Listening to) the Wrong Voice

Do you think that young people are the only ones that hear (listen to) the wrong voice? No. Sometimes, we as "seasoned" Christians do too. Satan's job is to steal, kill, and destroy God's people. No matter what it takes to get the job done, Satan will use anyone or anything to stop the Move of God. When we tear down our young people, they will come back fighting, not the enemy, but each other. We must not let Satan influence our thinking regarding our youth. We may think they don't listen, they're disrespectful or they're wasting our time, but we need to be steadfast and unmovable when it comes to dealing with them. They don't realize how much they need us. We have to realize that we need them as well. They are our future; and where would we be when we have to depend on them to care for us?

We as leaders in the Body of Christ must teach our youth to hear the right voice and that is the Voice of God. To know God is to love Him and to love Him is to know Him for God is Love. The question is: Do you know yourself? Mark 8:36 – "*What profit a man to gain the whole world and lose his own soul?*" Satan knows the Word so we must train our youth to know it also, and help them to hear and understand the Voice of God in this hour. For we wrestle not against flesh and blood, but against spiritual wickedness in high places. The enemy is all around and we have to be able to know the Voice of the Father when we hear it and respond accordingly. The way to know the Voice of God is to study and meditate on His word. We must impress upon our youth that they cannot develop a relationship with anyone unless they spend time with him/her. But we cannot teach this truth to our youth if we do not know it for ourselves.

The Word of God says: "*Greater is He that is in me then he that is in the world*" (1 John 4:4). We must live in the world and not of it (John 17:16). Before we can teach our youth how to discern between the voices, we must be rooted and grounded in God's Word. Young people are very intelligent. They know when we know and when we don't know. They can tell the difference between when we're real or not. We have to make sure we are hearing and following the right voices for ourselves. What voice have you heard in this great hour? I tell you the truth: It is better to be the sent one of Jesus Christ our Lord. Even Christ was tempted by Satan, who is the father of lies, but withheld Himself from any temptation given to men (Matthew 4:1-11).

Young people need to know that hearing (listening to) the wrong voice can stop the very plan and purpose that God has for our lives. God will allow us to be tempted by the enemy, but He will give us a way out of them all. When we are in disobedience, we can stop the plan that God has for our lives. We know that God does not bless any mess. I am amazed how many people allow the tricks of the enemy to get them out of position. How much longer will we listen to the voice of the devil tell us: *You cannot make it? No one loves you. Why don't you go ahead and die? They really don't care about you. See, you are all by yourself.*

The only way we hear the wrong voice is when a bad seed has been planted; and the door to our heart is open to the wrong word. This can mean only one thing: that we have been misused and abused, and rejection has overpowered our hearts. We must reshape the way our youth are thinking. The way to do that is a renewing of the mind. Romans 12:2 – *"And be not conformed to this world: but be ye transformed by the renewing of your mind, that ye may prove what is that good, and acceptable, and perfect, will of God."*

Satan and his demons wait in line to cause our youth to stumble. If he can inject them with self-doubt, low self-esteem, hatred, pity, perversion, guilt, blame, accusing of the brother, back biting, jealousy, envy, and pride, he can destroy our youth by leading them to self destruction. This can happen by listening to the wrong voice.

Satan went into the wilderness to stop the mission of Jesus Christ but was unsuccessful because Jesus was determined to follow and hear the Voice of His Father God. It is up to us to hear the right voice that will lead us to the truth, which is the Word of God. Hebrews 13:5b, 6 - *"…[F]or he hath said, I will never leave thee, nor forsake thee…So that we may boldly say, The Lord is my helper, and I will not fear what man shall do unto me."*

What voice are you hearing? God's Word says: *"Who hath believed our report and to whom is the arm of the LORD revealed?"* (Isaiah 53:1). We, the Church, shall believe the report of the Lord. If God said it, it is so. John 8:32 - ***"And ye shall know the*** *truth, and the truth shall make you free."* Ephesians 4:15 - *"But speaking the truth in love may grow up into him in all things, which is the head..."*

If we confess, believe, and receive the truth of God, we will be delivered and set free from the bondages of this world. Let's help the children of God know the truth by living a lifestyle that is pleasing to our Father in Heaven. Let's allow ourselves to be used by God and not man. The right way is YAHWEH and YAHWWEH is God. Philippians 4:8 – *"Finally, brethren, whatsoever things are true, whatsoever things are honest, whatsoever things are just, whatsoever things are pure, whatsoever things are lovely, whatsoever things are of good report; if there be any virtue, and if there be any praise, think on these things."*

We must impress upon our youth to think on the things of God, focus on Him and His Will for their lives. We are to impart in their lives that they are the children of light and that they have *A Voice to Be Heard* through the power and authority of Jesus Christ our Lord.

Stand up and hear the Voice of the Lord who is strong in power and mighty in battle. Learn to hear what the Spirit of God is saying to you right now. Watch and pray. Be alert to the surroundings of your youth. Make real sure that all of your leaders and volunteers are hearing the right voice. God's Word says test the Spirit by the Spirit: 1 John 4:1 – *"Beloved, believe not every spirit, but try the spirits whether they are of God: because many false prophets are gone out into the world."* God's Voice said, **"Let there be..."** and it was (Genesis 1). Now that's the voice we need to be hearing (listening to). If it does not line up with the Word of God, then it is not from God.

# A Cry Out for Troubled Teens

How many times have we overlooked the cry of a troubled teen? Teens are crying aloud all over the world. How many in the Body of Christ have heard the cry? The majority of our teens are in serious trouble because of peer pressure and the lack of communication in their homes. Troubled teens are all around us and it seems the Church is nowhere to be found. Our teens need to get into the church, but that can't and won't happen until the church gets into our teens. Youth leaders must develop more outreach activities to reach our youth. Once we get them involved, we must nurture them and teach them how to handle the many challenges they face on a daily basis.

So many homes have troubled teens and children in them, that it has become the norm in just about every family. The issues teens currently face have become so commonplace that it's accepted without question. Teen pregnancy is glamorized and sensationalized by society, exploiting our children on show after "Who's Your Baby Daddy?" show. Sexual immorality is expressed through the latest dance at the high school prom and even those who have been entrusted to teach our children have hit a new low by abusing them in the name of love.

We have got to raise our standards for our youth. We cannot choose to close our ears and shut our eyes to what's happening in our world. Our youth are in trouble and it's up to us to help them. If we abandon them now, we will all be in trouble because our future, the future of this world, will be in their hands.

We cannot be so busy, wrapped up in doing our own thing —in our church, our homes and our schools—that we fail to see the signs and hear the cry of our youth. An unheard cry from a troubled teen leads them to do things they normally would not even think of doing, just to get attention from anyone who is willing to give it to them. Most times that attention is not the kind they really need. Our young people are truly starving for love, acceptance, and compassion and these days, no one is at home to give it to them. We are failing our children as parents, mentors, leaders, teachers, and pastors. We have forsaken or forgotten all the principles and teaching of our fore-parents. We are too caught up in living and not paying attention to the lives of our youth. Our young people desperately need us and they need us now! Does this sound urgent? Well, it is! We cannot afford to wait any longer. We cannot put our youth to the side anymore. We have to quickly step up and pull them back in. We have allowed the world to take over our youth and the results are frightening.

Our teens are not feeling the love that is supposed to come from their parents and their church family. Society has labeled our children as troubled teens without hope and heading for destruction. They slap our young men in jail without so much as a second glance, and our young women are exploited at every turn. It seems no one is there to rescue them. It appears no one is there to care for them. So it is no wonder they feel like nobody cares what happens to them. The teen suicide rate[6] is getting worse along with sexual immorality, drugs, smoking, and alcohol abuse, murder, stealing, and lying among many other things that are keeping our teens in bondage. They do all this to escape the pain of rejection and the feeling of not being truly loved the way that they should be loved. Our world has evolved so much, and everyone is trying to get his/her piece of the pie. While there is nothing wrong with trying to get ahead, we have allowed acquiring things to become more important than what truly matters to God, and that is taking care of our children. Love is what we need to focus on. Love for the Father and love for each other is what is required of us and should be our first priority. When love prevails, we will hear the voices of our children and not only hear, but respond to their cries.

Man of God. Woman of God. Please pay attention. Now is the time for us to stand up and reclaim our youth. We have allowed the world to dictate how we raise and teach our children. God wants us to "train them up" in His way. Satan is on *his* job; which is to steal, kill, and destroy our children's lives. The evil one continues to poison their minds and thoughts with lies and deception and any damnable thing that can be imagined; and our children are open to it because there are no other choices available to them. We must provide a better choice for them. The choice between life and death is set before them and they don't even know it.

The Church is supposed to be set apart from the world and its cares. Mark 4:18-19 - "*And these are they which are sown among*

---

[6]   **Teen suicide** is the 3rd leading cause of death among young adults and adolescents 15 to 24 years of age (Anderson and Smith 2003). See **References** for the suicide prevention helpline.

*thorns; such as hear the word,* <sup>19</sup> *And the cares of this world, and the deceitfulness of riches, and the lusts of other things entering in, choke the word, and it becometh unfruitful."* Instead, we have shut the door on what really matters to God. God values His people and He always hears the cry of His children. Body of Christ, let us refocus our attention to the things of God and reach out to our youth. We have lost our sense of direction when we began focusing on mega-churches instead of saving mega souls. We failed to stay connected to the Word of God. STOP. Has the Church become like the world, only thinking about what they have obtained and become to man, and forgotten about God? Without God we will fail and our youth will fail if we fail.

The Church needs to begin demonstrating the Love of God and put their focus on what is important to God, and that is PEOPLE. Remember God's will is for none to perish (Matthew 18:14). His word in Matthew 18:6 says: *"**But whoso shall offend one of these little ones which believe in me, it were better for him that a millstone were hanged about his neck, and that he were drowned in the depth of the sea.**"* The Church has stopped seeking souls for the Father by any means necessary. So we need to come back to the Love of the Father and spread it abroad to all teens that are facing a serious crisis. There is a cry out for help in a time of trouble.

There are no big I's or little u's, so let's stop "tripping" and become a part of the solution and not the problem. Time is out for "They didn't call my name," or "Nobody even said thank you for what I did." God has given us a commandment to go into the entire world and teach all nations (Matthew 28:19). It is our responsibility in our churches and communities, to teach this generation about the Word of Christ Jesus, and to stand on His promises. In turn, we will see a generation become so radical and bold for Christ that they will begin to spread the Gospel of Jesus Christ our Lord to all that will hear.

Yes, let's begin to hear the cry out from our troubled teens and encourage, equip, impact, empower, and train our future leaders, *today*.

# Does Anyone Care About Me?

So many of our children around the world are asking this very question: *Does anyone care about me?* If we look at the condition of our world today regarding our children, it's no wonder so many are asking this question. Society has let it be made known that we don't have time for OPCs (Other People's Children).

We live in a society where children are faced with taking care of themselves and their siblings, not really understanding why this is happening to them and forcing them to make adult decisions in a world of chaos. In this world today, there are so many absent parents that the states are forced to take care of unwanted children. It is a place where grandparents and great-grandparents are trying to raise a generation that is full of rejection, hurt, and pain because of confused and lost parents who can't or won't live for Christ. These children are forced to grow up before their time; and we wonder why the kids in this world are "too grown."

Other children in third world countries are saying that many Christians come and give, but very little love is found. They say: "*We do get many things that come our way, but without compassion. Does anyone care about me? Time after time, we have died in someone's arms only for them to feel sorry about the condition they are seeing. We are looking for an answer for I am hungry, I am naked, and I am sick and without any hope. Does anyone care about me?*"

What a sad, sad, commentary! How awful for any child to feel this way. We have failed to hear the cry of our children because of our own selfish desires, putting anything and anyone before them. Oh, how we have failed to realize that it takes a village, a community, and devoted Christians to take a stand and say, "Our children need us." We must hear the cry that is going on all over this world, a cry out for help.

Would you believe there are many Christian homes with Christian parents where the children are feeling the same rejection, hurt, and pain that the children of the world are feeling? We allow our children to wear clothes that are too revealing and allow them to listen to all kinds of *garbage* they call music. We, as Christians must be delivered from a spirit called *Religion* and pay attention to the cry of the many youths in the Body of Christ. Can you say: Too heavenly minded to be any earthly good?

If we hear our children cry and show them that we care by helping them find their place in the Body of Christ, what an awesome Move of God will come forth that will impact our children. Proverbs 22:6 tell us to train them. If we fail to heed the cry of our youth, we will be facing a crisis in the Body of Christ with this generation and generations to come, because if we do not train this generation, who will train the next?

Time after time, we hear adults speak of this "lost generation," but what have we done to help them reach their greatest potential in life. Matthew 12:36-37 tell us that we will be held accountable for every idle word that comes out of our mouths.

Building big churches is fine, but if we don't have the next generation to continue the work that was accomplished, one might say that all of this hard work was done in vain, and will die right along with the builders.

Let's stop speaking death into our children's and youths' lives, and empower them with the truth which is the Word of God. God never wanted any of us to put other things ahead of winning a soul. Guess what? Every child, youth, and teen has a soul that is valuable to God and it should also be like that with every believer in the Body of Christ. Every battle that needs to be won is won with the Lord on our side. If God be for us, who can be against us? (Romans 8:31).

We need to see our youth and ourselves as God truly sees His people. In story after story in the Bible, God encourages His people by showing them the good He sees in them and calling them out to operate as He sees them. It is time for parents, leaders, and individuals to see as God sees and call out the good in our children, and impact and empower their lives to greatness. Just think about it, if God saw the good in each of us, why do we allow the evil one to keep us from seeing the good in someone else? I am a firm believer that what we do for others will be done unto us, for the Word of God says you shall reap what you sow (Job 4:8). Are you sowing any good seeds in the life of a child?

Many families are on the edge with their children. They have forgotten how to raise a child in these days - sometimes due to the stress of trying to make ends meet. I believe the reason we have forgotten is we have not held onto the teachings of our fore-parents. The Word of God tells us everything we need, but we have forsaken the spoken Word of God. Some parents do not want to be parents any longer; some really don't know how. The new trend is to be friends with kids because this will keep them young. Our children need more than just things; they need instruction, nurturing, love, and guidance. In some cases, the parents aren't much older than the child.

It is time for the Body of Christ—every believer—to demonstrate the Love of God. Romans 5:8 – *"But God commendeth his love toward us, in that, while we were yet sinners, Christ died for us."* We must help give our children a sense of hope by speaking words of encouragement to everyone that God allows us to come in contact with during our time on earth. Then we will become a "We Care" people for the whole world to see. Remember, we must be able to hear their cry and answer the question: *Does anyone care about me?* Just say, "Yes, we do care." And if God values people, we should also do the same.

# Who Really Loves Me?

*"Yes, Jesus loves me! Yes, Jesus loves me! Yes, Jesus loves me! The Bible tells me so."*[7]

So often people don't realize that our youth are questioning who really loves them. Just like some adults, we must understand that God sent His Son Jesus, to show us His greatest love. The love of man is nothing compared to God's Love, for God loves unconditionally each and every one of His children. John 13:34 – *"**A new commandment I give unto you, That ye love one another; as I have loved you, that ye also love one another.**"*

John 15:13 – *"**Greater love hath no man than this, that a man lay down his life for his friends.**"*

John 3:16 - *"**For God so Loved the world, that he gave his only begotten Son, that whosoever believeth in him should not perish, but have everlasting life.**"*

---

[7]  "Jesus Loves Me" Hymn (Anna Bartlett Warner, 1859)

John 14:15-16, 18, 21 -

*"If ye love me, keep my commandments."*
*"And I will pray the Father, and he shall give you another comforter, that he may abide with you for ever..."*
*"I will not leave you comfortless: I will come to you...."*
*"He that hath my commandments, and keepeth them, he it is that loveth me: and he that loveth me shall be loved of my Father, and I will love him, and will manifest myself to him."*

Romans 5:8 - *"But God commendeth his love toward us, in that, while we were yet sinners, Christ died for us."*

If our youth don't feel loved, they really cannot understand the Love of the Father or their parents or loved ones. Our youth need to be reassured that they are loved more than they can imagine. You have those who do not even love themselves, so how can they give love to anyone else? It's time for us to rebuild, renew, and reestablish our way of thinking. God's Word says love covers a multitude of sin (1 Peter 4:8). 1 John 4:11, 20-21 - *"Beloved, if God so loved us, we ought also to love one another...If a man say, I love God, and hateth his brother, he is a liar: for he that loveth not his brother whom he hath seen, how can he love God whom he hath not seen? And this commandment have we from him, That he who loveth God love his brother also."*

Our command is to show the Love of God that is in Christ Jesus to everyone we come in contact with daily. We must reinvest our lives to our children so they can know the Love of the Father, and to help them realize that God's love is real.

It is important that we assure our young people that if no one ever says to them that they are loved, God loves them first and His love will never end. What an awesome feeling to know that the Love of the Father lasts forever. People who do not love themselves cannot and will not be able to love others. God's love is unconditional. All we must do is receive it and be obedient to spread the Word of God to all we meet. Who really loves me? God does, and so do I.

# Help in the Time of Trouble

**H** ELP US

**E** NPOWER OUR FUTURE

**L** EADERS WITH BOLDNESS AND

**P** OWER PROPHETICALLY

When our youth cry out in time of trouble, we must be able to hear their voices. So many people have the mentality of not responding to the needs of young people. Some think they are to be seen and not heard. Others think that they are acting out only to be seen and heard, but very few understand the cry of a troubled youth. The time is now for us to not only *see* them, but we must also *hear* their cries for help.

We must be able to put more focus on troubled teens and youths whenever they come into our presence. Fasting and praying for our youth on a daily basis will help us hear from the Throne Room of God. Then we will be able to sense when something is not right when they come into our presence.

Jesus knew when trouble was around Him. We must learn to hear from God in a very quick way. This is hearing from God's Holy Spirit and using the discernment that each one of us is given through the Word of God.

Build up a relationship with your youth so that you can get to know them and learn who they are, so when something is not right with them you will be able to notice it right away. Don't pretend with them, for they *do* know when people are real. One step you can take in building a relationship with your youth is not to focus on the big things in their lives, but focus on the little things first. You will see a relationship forming without even following them around. Young people will attach themselves to you if they can trust you with the little things. Then they won't have a problem with sharing the big things that affect their lives.

Don't forget that kids are people too, they bleed, they cry, and they hurt just like you. Peer pressure plays a great part in our youths' lives today. Everybody wants to be somebody, other than being him or herself. Just remember that peer pressure in everyday life is no joke. Some of our youth will fall into temptation, whether it is drugs, alcohol or sexual sin. It happens to the best of them.

If a youth is experiencing trouble at home, believe me when I say, the only escape they have is a youth group at church where they can seek help in time of trouble. If they are not part of a youth group in the church, and they seek help in the church and no one hears or sees their cry for help, they will be lost in time of trouble. Learn to hear the cry of a troubled child. You could help save a life.

If they don't get the help they need, youth will find other alternatives to cope with their problems. They may become part of a gang or run away from home, or they will consider or commit suicide. If young people are never taught to release the pressures of everyday life, or the proper way to deal with the stresses they encounter with being a youth of today, they will never know how to do it on their own. They will most likely fall deeper into temptation and pride, and eventually not seek help in time of trouble. Ephesians 6:11 – *"Put on the whole armor of God, that ye may be able to stand against the wiles of the devil."*

Some youth are saying: *Where is God in time of trouble?* Are you telling them that He is right here? Hebrews 13:5b and 6 says God will never leave you nor forsake you and that the Lord is our helper. These are two great assurances that God gives to us in time of trouble. God said it. I believe it, and it is so.

Let's build up our youth in this generation, helping them become empowered with the power of God. Encourage and equip your youth, and put on the Armor of God.[8]

---

[8] Read Joshua 1:9 and Ephesians 6:10-18

# Do You Know Who You Are?

It is so important to know who you are. We must instill in our youth as children of the King to know who they really are in Christ Jesus. The Church has a great opportunity to help train our future leaders. In everything we do and say, we must encourage, build up, and empower them with the Word of God. If we don't know who we are, we will become lost to the Will of God for our lives. We must teach our youth to know God first, then to know who they are in Christ Jesus.

We were bought with a price. The precious blood of God's only begotten Son, Jesus Christ our Lord paid it all for us to be children and heirs of the Most High God. When we become something we were not meant to be, we lose all sense of the direction God's word has given mankind to follow.

What are you becoming? Are you becoming something you were not meant to be? Are you reaching for something you were not meant to have? We have a tendency to become something we are not meant to be. We are trying to get things that were meant for someone else. Knowing yourself is so important. Who are you? Do you really know or are you pretending to be someone else?

It is not only important to know who you are, but WHOSE you are. To know God is to know *whose* we are - and look not, to the left nor to the right, but "*look to the hill which cometh your help*" (Psalm 121:1), for our help comes from the Lord. Our Father will withhold nothing from us if we only ask in His name.

We must look into the mirror of our hearts and see whose we are indeed. God knows our ending before our beginning. Why do we try to please man all the time instead of pleasing and obeying the Maker, God the Father, who created us? We are priests and kings in God's eyesight. When will we take our rightful place in the Body of Christ and stop following after the things of this world?

Don't get out of position with the Will of God. Young people need to know that they can make a difference in the Body of Christ. We allow people—old and young—to take us out of our position. When the enemy comes in—which are the devil and his evil army—we must flee from their influence. They will try on every hand to disconnect us from our life source, Jesus Christ our Lord.

Thank God for His GRACE and NEW MERCIES every day. When we, as believers repent and give it all to God, then He can change us from the inside out and deliver us from the evil one, even if it is ourselves. We must remind ourselves what the Word of God says, that He shall supply all our needs according to His riches in glory (Philippians 4:19).

Knowing who you are will bring you into the presence of our Father. Inform our youth that when they know who they really are, they can go forth with power and boldness to accomplish the plan that God has for their lives.

Teach our youth that they are more than conquerors (Romans 8:37) in Christ. They must be led by the Spirit and inherit the good of the land. To love Him is to know Him, but to love you is to know Him that loves you first (John 3:16; Romans 8:5; 1 John 4:7-11).

We have the blessed assurance that Jesus is ours. Wherever we go, if we know God's word and do His will, He promises in His word never to leave us nor forsake us and that the Lord is our helper (Hebrews 13:5-6). What awaits us is better than what we see in the natural, if our FOCUS is on JESUS.

Know who you are and inherit the Kingdom of God!

# Do You Know Him?

Most of our youth in the Body of Christ do not know who God is —the Father, the Son, and the Holy Spirit—for themselves. Leadership must help their youth develop a personal relationship with God. In the majority of our youths' homes, there is no talk about having a relationship with God or study of His word. It is vitally important that youth understand that a relationship with God is needed in order to know Him. Many people know *of* Him, but it is important to know Him for yourself. As a leader, you must get to know your youth to find out how much they know about God, giving you an indication of where they need to begin in their journey to discover who God really is, and how important it is for them to make Him a major part of their lives. [9]

When young people come to our churches, we make the mistake and assume they know something about God and His creation, but sadly, many do not. So the first thing we must do is assess their knowledge to see how much they actually know. You must start at the beginning. You cannot teach them who God is by quoting King James Version scripture and "preaching down

---

[9] Read the book of Genesis the first and second chapter.

the house." You have to meet them where they are. Take baby steps, because it's just like giving a baby a bottle. You wouldn't give a baby meat, would you? So be careful not to overwhelm your youth.

You have to gently guide them into the acceptance that they are sinners in need of help from someone. Then they need to know that there is someone who can help them with any and everything they need. Explain to them that because He loves them so much, God sent His only Son to die for them so that they can live with Him forever in heaven. Let them know that God will reveal Himself to whosoever wants to know Him. He gives all of us a free will to serve Him, and to seek after Him through His word. Help your youth to understand that God has a purpose and plan for each of their lives and that we were chosen by Him before the foundation of this earth.

The most important task is to allow them to follow the Word of God with a Teen Study Bible[10] so that each one can read His word in a way that may be more understandable to them. Proverbs 3:5-6 is among many scriptures that can help them to fully understand who He is to us and for us. God is our Heavenly Father who created us for His own purpose. Let your youth know that God gave them a desire to know more. Discourage any embarrassment they may feel for not knowing how to read a Bible or not being able to find scripture quickly. Let them know it's not a matter of quantity, but quality. The more they read and study, the more they will know about God and His will for their lives.

---

[10] **Teens Study Bible**: KJV Axis: A Study Bible for Teens (2007, Thomas Nelson publisher)

Let your youth know that God will not force anyone to serve Him or make them know who He is. He will, however, send people into the lives of those willing to learn of Him, and as they learn about the Father, they will also learn about the Son and the Holy Spirit, for they are one in the Trinity.

Many youth learn the ways of the world quickly but don't put much effort in knowing the Word of God like they should. We must ask ourselves what is wrong with that picture. Part of the answer might be the way in which you present the subject of God to your youth. Learning about God should be exciting. It shouldn't always be fire and brimstone; and it shouldn't be trivialized either, but presented to youth in a way they can relate to. Bringing the Word of God to the youth should start in the home, but if it doesn't, we must be ready to help each youth find out who God is. They must understand that without a relationship with God, they cannot have eternal life. Explain to them that just like they wouldn't live with a stranger, God lives with those eternally whom He knows and who know Him.

Knowing God requires a personal relationship with Him, which starts with understanding that believing and obeying His word will keep us in His will. God said in His word that they will know Him by your love one toward another (John 13:35). It is important to live your life so that others will see God in you and glorify the Father who is in heaven.

We must teach this generation that the way to know Him is through His word, and it is critical how we live our lives in front of our youth, children, and teens. To know Him is to love Him and to love Him is to know Him.

Leaders, please don't become so blinded by what, who or how *you* know Him that you lose a generation of youth that do not understand how to know Him for themselves. Don't be so holy that your youth cannot approach you without you trying to correct something they've said or done. That attitude can cause the door to shut on your youth, or place them in captivity without really teaching them that Christ Jesus died for all sins.

We need to be faithful and dedicated individuals in the Body of Christ, to focus on reaching and impacting a generation that only wants someone to be real with them in every area of their lives. In order for our youth to know God the way that they should, we must be open and willing to hear the cry of our youth and build a generation that only wants to hear the truth - a generation that can recognize a lie and immediately call the enemy out. Jesus said in the Word of God that the truth should make you free (John 8:32); and whom the Son sets free is free indeed.

When leaders really know Christ, they can in turn teach and equip our future leaders—our youth—to know Him. Then everyone can join in the battle, helping to reach their peers with the Word of God. Once our youth get on fire for the Lord, there is no turning back for them. They will be radical and persistent in helping to save a dying generation of youth. The saying remains the same, "each one reach one" until all have heard the Voice of God.

Our youth hear so many promises that are quickly broken, but this generation is looking for a different sound; and it must be one that can impact and empower them to go forth with power and authority, and take this world by force. Now is the time for generals in the Body of Christ to teach, to equip, and to train future leaders so that they won't be afraid to fight to the end.

# A Way Out

Most of our youth are looking for a way out of everyday trials and tribulations due to situations beyond their control. The Word of God says that there is a way that seems right to a man but the end is destruction (Proverbs 14:12).

But the hope we have is in John 14:6, Jesus said, "*I am the way, the truth, and the life: no man cometh unto the Father, but by me.*" We need to begin to teach our youth how to trust in God no matter what the problem or situation might be looking like at time of trouble.

God has given His creation a way out, but it is really up to every individual to receive the gift of salvation. The Word of God is the only way we have out of our sinful nature. Sin separates us from the Father forever (Isaiah 59:2).

A way out is a choice we make in hearing the Voice of God, for He is calling us out of darkness into His marvelous light (1 Peter 2:9). Please encourage your youth so that they will know that no matter what situations might be going on in their lives, there is a way out. We do not want the enemy to tell them that no one loves them or that they don't really have a way out. We don't want them to feel like no one cares if they live or die, or feel that they should take the enemy's way out and kill themselves to be free.

We must be willing to teach them the Word of God by showing scriptures like Hebrews 13:5-6. Impress upon them *again* that God will *never* leave them nor forsake them, and the Lord is our helper in time of trouble. Allowing them to know and understand that trials and tribulations come in like a flood, but we must lift up the standard, which is the Word of God, and remember that God's will is for none to perish (Matthew 18:14). How awesome is it to encounter the mercies and Grace of God through His word?

If we fail to encourage and empower their lives with the Word of God by demonstrating a way out, most likely our youth will fall into a lifestyle of drugs, sexual behavior, lying and stealing, cursing, and only God knows what else. Teach them from the Word of God that there is now no condemnation for those who are in Christ Jesus. We must tell them to fall back into the hands of an Almighty God and receive the way out through His forgiven word.

Do you know what way out that your youth are taking in a world of chaos? We make everything so hard; but don't you know, it is very simple if we only trust and obey the Word of God. We must not just trust anyone, but trust the Voice of God through His servants, whether they are pastors, teachers, parents or youth leaders. Proverbs 3:5-6 – "*Trust in the Lord with all thine heart; and lean not unto thine own understanding. In all thy ways acknowledge him, and he shall direct thy paths.*" 1 Corinthians 10:13 – "*There hath no temptation taken you but such as is common to man: but God is faithful, who will not suffer you to be tempted above that ye are able; but will with the temptation also make a way to escape, that ye may be able to bear it."*

God will show us a way out through His chosen people who walk in obedience. Hear this: Without God in our lives there is no way out of a burning hell. We can do nothing without God the Father who created everything that is good.

The way out of any trouble is just to trust in the plan and purpose God has for each of our lives as a believer. The world is crying aloud for a way out and we are the Christ that most of them will ever see. Let's help hear the voices of our youth by showing them that there is a way out that can change the course of each of their lives, from a life of destruction to a life of instruction, through the power of Jesus Christ our Lord. He can change us from the inside out. They need to know that the BIBLE is the basic instructions before leaving earth, full of God's love and power.

Say yes to the Lord, and go beyond the normal situation to empower your youth to become motivated to show other youth a way out.

# Who Will Pray for Me?

PRAYER is a powerful tool that is given to us by our Father God. If the evil one (the devil) could keep us away from prayer he would. Prayer is simply talking to God. Many of our children, parents, and guardians do not understand the power of prayer.

Many of our youth are asking the question: *Who will pray for me?* It is unfortunate, but we must be honest and face the fact that a majority of youths' households don't even conduct prayer on a daily basis. How can they learn prayer when no one at home is praying for them or each other? When fear grips our youth, prayer is the key, along with comforting them and teaching them through the Word of God that they are not alone (Hebrews 13:5-6). In all of thy getting get an understanding (Proverbs 3:5-6).

Our youth urgently need our prayers. Who should pray for them? We all should be praying down God's mercies and blessings upon these innocent children, mothers, fathers, mentors, pastors, teachers, brothers, and sisters. Those who do the Will of the Lord should pray without ceasing. Luke 18:1 – *"And he (Jesus) spake a parable unto them to this end, that men ought always to pray, and not to faint."*

Let's take this a step further. When a baby is in the womb of his or her mother, that child should be prayed for everyday by someone who knows the power of prayer. An intercessor is someone who goes to God on behalf of another. Their job is to stay on their knees before the Lord for God's people around the world, praying with fervent prayer (James 5:16).

Jesus is a prime example of praying for us continually without ceasing. The Word also tells us that the Holy Spirit makes intercession on our behalf. Romans 8:26 – "*Likewise the Spirit also helpeth our infirmities: for we know not what we should pray for as we ought: but the Spirit itself maketh intercession for us with groaning which cannot be uttered.*"

The power of prayer is awesome. You cannot live victoriously without it. If we follow Christ as Christ followed His Father, we will fulfill everything that God gave in His word for His sons and daughters to do. Prayer is a powerful tool that can move mountains, open blind eyes, heal the sick, and raise the dead. Prayer can open or close doors, enable you to receive food for the hungry and shelter for the homeless. When everything in the natural fails, pray to the Father for He can do everything *but* fail.

In order for you to have effective prayer, you must have FAITH. Prayer and faith operate hand-in-hand. For without faith, it is impossible to please God—who rewards them that diligently seek after Him (Hebrews 11:6). When the question comes up regarding who will pray for me, just remember to be aware of the concerns that our little ones have. Reassure them that Jesus, the Holy Spirit, the pastor, the leaders, and many intercessors from around the world who truly hear from God will be praying on their behalf. Remember, "*The effectual, fervent prayer of the righteous shall availeth much*" (James 5:16).

# Intercessory Prayer for Teens

God has called each of us to do a very specific job. We must take what the Word of God says and apply it to every area of our lives. We must be unified and focused on loving each other without conditions. 1 John 4:7 - *"Beloved, let us love one another: for love is of God; and every one that loveth is born of God, and knoweth God."*

Prayer is vital to the success of any ministry (1 Timothy 2:1-8). Intercessors are a very integral part of every ministry. They are the ones who are on the front line in the WAR. They are the air attack, striking by sending prayers up to heaven on behalf of teens, youth, pastors, leaders, nations, and the church family. This is a job not to be taken lightly. They are the forerunners, just as John the Baptist was in Jesus' time. We should be the same. James 5:16 - *"Confess your faults one to another, and pray one for another, that ye may be healed. The effectual fervent prayer of a righteous man availeth much."*

Intercessors must have a passion—*an intense love, desire, eagerness of emotion*—to move in intercession. It is a representation of Christ's passion. A true intercessor must be Christ-minded and one in the Spirit, and one in the Lord. An intercessor must definitely FOCUS on what the Spirit is telling them to do in order to intercede on another's behalf. Our youth must be on one accord with the Move of God. An intercessor's heart must be set on obeying God's voice through His Spirit. We must understand, and more importantly *believe*, that as intercessors, things happen when we pray.

Prayer is one of the keys that will unlock heaven on behalf of God's people. When we teach our youth this principle, we will inherit a generation that will be willing to fall on their faces in prayer.

The Word of God teaches that there are effective ways to pray. Here are some things to keep in mind when teaching youth to pray in Spiritual warfare:

1. **Pray In the Name of Jesus**
2. **Plead the Blood of Jesus**
3. **Pray the Word of God**
4. **Allow the Holy Spirit to make Intercession through us by the using of tongues in our heavenly language.**
5. **Be BOLD and courageous in our prayers**
6. **Put on the whole ARMOR (Ephesians 6:10-18)**

Intercessory prayer is a powerful tool for any individual. True intercessors will hear the Voice of God. God has given us His Son Jesus and The Holy Spirit to intercede on our behalf. We, as a church, need to impact and impart in our future leaders. We must be willing to train up young people ready for WAR and not afraid to be radical for the Lord.

Intercessory prayer is warring on behalf of our youth and others to reach the Throne Room of Heaven where God is seated. Our youth of today need much training for tomorrow's trials and tribulations. We must speak to them and show them—in the Word of God—that they come to make us strong.

Let's not sit and do nothing regarding our youth, but get up and train this generation that will be *radical* and not be ashamed of where God is taking them in the Spirit of the Lord. When they become on *fire* for the Lord there will be nothing that can ever stop them once they have been trained and released to do the work of the Lord.

It's time to teach, impart, and to train our youth. What time is it? IT'S YOUTH TIME. We need to get busy and prepare our youth to change this world with the *power* and *fire* of the Lord.

Just think, if we can help develop our youth and bring out what is already inside of them, what an awesome and powerful ministry they will have impacting and reaching other like-minded youth all over the world.

Intercessory prayer is needed in the Body of Christ because this tool will allow us, the Body of Christ, to enter into a whole other dimension. The Word of God tells us: *"My people are destroyed for lack of knowledge"* (Hosea 4:6). II Chronicles 7:14 - *"If my people, which are called by my name, shall humble themselves, and pray, and seek my face, and turn from their wicked ways; then will I hear from heaven, and will forgive their sin, and will heal their land."*

The Word of God tells us in 1 Peter 5:8 to "*Be sober (be on the alert), be vigilant; because your adversary the devil, as a roaring lion, walketh about, seeking whom he may devour.*" Guess what? We already know who has the victory!

Just remember, our assignment to the Body of Christ is to train up an army of warriors equipped and prepared for WAR! Acts 10:34 – "*God is no respecter of person.*" What He does in us, He can do also in our youth!

Prayer leads to hearing from God, and hearing from God brings a breakthrough. God reveals prayer needs and gives strategies to overcome the enemy by His word. Victory will come through obedience to the Lord. 1 Samuel 15:22b – "*Behold, to obey* is *better than sacrifice, and to hearken than the fat of rams.*"

There are also some very important tools that we must use not only as children of God, but His very elect, such as the BIBLE, the concordance, and books regarding prayer and intercession prayer (*see reference*). We must never be ashamed of praying in the marketplace or anywhere that God has called us to go. 2 Timothy 4:2 - "*Be ye ready in season and out of season.*" We will never know who and what God is changing because of our prayers being sent to heaven, so just be obedient.

You have heard this saying from time to time: Prayer is talking and communicating with God, just like we would talk with our family, friends, and anyone else. We must establish a personal relationship with God, just like the relationships we have with our loved ones and friends in our circle of influences. It is all about the one who created everything, God our Father. Without a relationship and communication with God we will not be connected to the "Life Source" through Jesus Christ our Lord and Savior. A relationship with God would allow us to just talk about the many issues of our hearts and to intercede in prayer for those to whom we stand in the gap for to receive a life changing experience. Just watch the difference a prayer makes in the lives of others. Trust and obey.

Prayer is the key to communicating with God anytime, anyplace, and anywhere. Without the communication factor, we will not get our desires answered because we have not continued to pray without ceasing (1 Thessalonians 5:17). Teach the youth that it's ok to stand in the gap for their peers. We must train them to go beyond the veil and enter into His presence with thanksgiving and supplication unto the Father, making all requests known unto Him (Philippians 4:6). Remember, Jesus is the chief intercessor.

# A Chance to Be Forgiven

How do we feel when we realize that we have wronged a loved one? We say we're sorry and hope our apology is accepted. We may feel bad for days, regretting our words or actions; but once we are forgiven, we immediately begin to feel better. Everybody has sought forgiveness at some time during their life's journey, but sometimes we fail to forgive. Luke 6:37 and Colossians 3:13 talk about how we should forgive others as Jesus forgave us. Many children ask this question when they have fallen into the temptations of the evil one or in a rebellious state. Will I be forgiven by God? Yes you will be forgiven, but we must forgive as Christ forgave mankind. Jesus will not forgive us before His Father if we don't forgive each other. Matthew 6:14-15 - "*For if ye forgive men their trespasses, your heavenly Father will also forgive you. But if ye forgive not men their trespasses, neither will your Father forgive your trespasses.*"

Holding on to past wrongs done against us and refusing to forgive has a stronghold on many people in today's society. This very act will keep us from a chance to be with an Almighty God through eternal life.

Children seek the faces of a loving father and mother, waiting to be forgiven for the many times that they have messed up in school, home, church or other areas of their life journey. We all have gotten caught up in the moment and done things we may even be ashamed of, or lost all sense of direction and right standard. We have taken the many people that care for us on a roller-coaster ride of emotional drama. How do we forgive those who continue to hurt us time and time again? It is found in the Word of God. We must read and study the Word on a daily basis so when trouble comes, the Word of God will pour out of our hearts. We must understand that sometimes our youth do wrong just to get some attention. They think even negative attention is better than none at all. Please hear the voices of the youth crying out for help.

If we don't teach our youth to forgive, and if we don't forgive ourselves, it can turn into bitterness and eventually cause us to lose our souls when we don't repent and ask God's forgiveness. When teens, children, and our youth make a bad decision, please try to give them an understanding of forgiveness and try not to condemn them for that decision. Remember that God has forgiven all of us when we have made bad decisions in serving Him. Allow His word to cleanse us from all unrighteousness.

A chance to be forgiven is an awesome task that God has given each of us to live by through His precious word. We as parents, pastors, and leaders need to join forces to become a part of one of the greatest moves in the Body of Christ. The world needs to see the Body of Christ forgive those who trespass against them.[11]

---

[11]   Read Matthew 6:9-15

# A Covenant Letter With Teens, Volunteers and Staff Leaders

God made a covenant with Abraham, Noah and many of His people whom He has chosen to do His will. A covenant is an agreement, usually formal, between two or more persons to do or not do something specified. A covenant relationship is important in the Body of Christ. We must be responsible in our Christian journey. So many people have come in and out of the lives of our youth. What is your motivation for working with your youth? Are you willing to make a lifetime commitment or do you just want recognition? Are you seeking God's approval or the approval of man?

God's word tells us to "*seek first the kingdom of God and all these things will be added unto you*" (Matthew 6:33). How many people seek the face of others to hear a lie instead of seeking the truth in God's word? Well, many of us have fallen into this trap by seeking another source.

We must hold people accountable for their decisions. If God called you to deal with teens and youths in this ministry—or whatever ministry you are presently working with—be very sure you stay FOCUSED. So many people start the work with the youth ministry, but very few finish it. Youths need people who are willing to minister to their needs. We must show all leaders and volunteers up front that they will be held accountable by signing a covenant form committing them to a least one year of service to their ministry. We are aware of other things happening in our lives, but their creditability is at stake.

A covenant is very important for it shall test your character. God made a covenant with His people. When God destroyed the world the first time, He told Noah that a sign will be placed in the sky made by Him regarding the covenant (Genesis 9:15). It was a beautiful rainbow from God for the whole world to see. It is a sign of God's promise to us and we need to make and keep our promises to our youth.

If leaders and volunteers are committed, they will have no problem signing a covenant letter for at least one year. A commitment is a great model to teach the teens and youth to become future leaders. As they follow you, they will notice the commitment you have made to teach and equip them for their ministries.

When dealing with leaders and volunteers, be mindful to give them the rules and regulations, and post them for all to see. Don't forget to keep the standard in line: one for all and all for one. Let them know that God has never broken a covenant, but man has. So stay focused and try to do your best and let God do the rest. He will allow you to go from start to finish. It's a faith walk, trusting God's word. Whatever He tells you to do, just do it for His glory. Being committed to God is far better than being committed to the world.

## COVENANT LETTER

I, _____ *(your name here)* am willing to be in agreement with the _____ _____, *(your Church name here)* as a covenant member to help in the development of our future leaders by training, equipping or mentoring them according to the Word of God according to Proverbs 22:6. As a covenant member, my task is to continue the process of being trained and equipped for the work of this ministry. I am to build a relationship with those who are a part of this Body of Christ, through love, commitment, dedication, and trust. I will be faithful in Bible study, worship service, and other programs or activities that are a part of our Church and the community in which we serve, according to Matthew 28:19-20. I will keep the faith at all times by praying for the ministry vision and supporting the ministries with my tithes and offerings, according to Malachi 3:8-12. I will also give my time to this ministry. I will be mindful of being on time for every class, program, service or event held in the name of this church to the best of my ability. I am dedicated and accountable to the commitment I have made as part of this ministry. I pray for all leaders and the church congregation to hear the Voice of God in decision-making regarding church growth and Youth Ministry Department.

Signatures: _____ Date: _____
                        Volunteer


_____ Date: _____
                   Youth Leader


_____ Date: _____
          Youth Ministry Leader

God's Blessing upon your ministry!

# Elder Connita Lee

# REFERENCES

- The House of Prayer for All Nations Ministries, Chicago, Illinois

- The Holy Bible and Bible on the Web: King James Version & Amplified Bible

- The Youth Bible: New Century Version Word Group

- Intercessory Prayer by Dutch Sheets

- Praying Hyde by John Hyde

- Prayers That Rout Demons by Apostle John Eckhardt

- The Secret of Intercession by Andrew Murray

- Anderson RN, Smith BL. Teen Suicide. Deaths: leading causes for 2001. *National Vital Statistics Report* 2003; 52(9):1-86.

- Bartlett Warner, Anna. "Jesus Loves Me" Hymn, 1859.

- Fitzgerald, F. Scott. "The Curious Case of Benjamin Button" Short Story, 1921.

- Rodine M.Ed., Oman Ph.D., Vesley Ph.D., Aspy Ph.D., Tolma MPH, Ph.D., Marshall, Fluhr. Potential Protective Effects of the Community Involvement Asset on Adolescent Risk Behaviors. *Journal of Youth Development* 2006; Vol. 1, No. 1, Article 0601FA005

- Scriven, Joseph M. "What a Friend We Have in Jesus" Poem, 1855.

- Sinha, Canaan, Gelles 2007. Adolescent Risk Behaviors and Religion: Findings from a National Study. *Journal of Adolescence*, Volume 30, Issue 2, April 2007, page 231-249.

**If you or someone you know is having thoughts of suicide, contact the National Suicide Prevention Lifeline at 1-800-273-TALK (1-800-273-8255), or visit the website: http://www.suicidepreventionlifeline.org/**

# ABOUT THE AUTHOR

Connita Lee, the daughter of Marguerite E. Lee and the late Jesse J. Lee of Chicago, Illinois, is the seventh child of ten children. She is the adopted mother of her adopted son by faith Dennis E. Craig and the grandmother of two beautiful grandchildren: Dennis Keyon and Kayla Denise Craig. She has lived in Illinois all of her life and has always wanted to be a missionary to the nations.

Connita Lee was blessed by the Father to retire at the age of 47, on December 31, 2003 after working for over twenty-five years at Central States Pension Fund in Rosemont, Illinois. She celebrated her 50th Jubilee Birthday Celebration in August of 2006.

Connita Lee was blessed to travel to Europe for a month in 1988, visiting many nations before the call came to go and be a servant in Honduras and Africa. Elder Lee is known too many as Granny, Auntie Connita, and sister to the people in her family of faith. She is an Ordained Presbytery Elder at The House of Prayer For All Nations Ministries, Cell Group Leader, Director over Youth Ministry and she was an Overseer of Intercessors and Deliverance Ministry, and much more.

Elder Lee's calling is to impact and equip both our youth and the young at heart. She realizes the responsibility and purpose of training the next generation to walk in the destiny and calling that God has already prepared for their lives. Elder Lee has a great concern to develop a strategy to keep the youth involved in our churches today.

She is a Spiritual mom to those whom she has come in contact with and not just at her church, but around the world. They see her as a Mother of Zion. A woman of destiny and purpose, she only wants to fulfill the call to love God's people unconditionally and walk in obedience according to His word. Her name Connie or Connita means "Faithful" and she knows without a shadow of doubt that God has truly been to FAITHFUL in her life.

Elder Lee is a woman who wants to see the youth praise and worship God in their own way in the Body of Jesus Christ. Her current vision is to build a youth center in the Roseland (Chicago) community to reach our youth in this 21st century.

# AWARDS

**Elder Connita Lee has been a recipient of numerous awards including:**

- ❖ Certificate from Child Evangelism Fellowship
- ❖ I'M THIRD AWARD for <u>God First, Others Second, I'm Third</u> from Kid's Across America Camp for three consecutive years.
- ❖ LT. Governor's Youth Ambassador Award
- ❖ L.C.C.D Caring Servant Award: from the "Lutheran Congregation for Career Development".
- ❖ Ladies Aide of Faith Award

❖ Youth Ministry Award: for developing the "Straight Talk" strategy.

❖ Certificate of Achievement Award from Central States Pension Fund

❖ Certificate of Completion - Leadership training for the Prophetic Training and Activation from the New Vision of Faith Fellowship.

❖ Certificate of Appreciation - Award for Eldership at the House of Prayer for All Nations Ministries

Printed in the United States
150809LV00004BB/4/P

9 781438 979250